Cold Cases: Solved

Volume 5

18 Fascinating

True Crime Cases

Robert Keller

**Please Leave Your Review of This Book at
http://bit.ly/kellerbooks**

ISBN: 9798366173704

© 2022 by Robert Keller

robertkellerauthor.com

Table of Contents

Purgatory

Michael Boucher

In the small town of West Gardiner, Maine, in the early 1970s, the Dill family was living an idyllic life. The six siblings and their parents were exceptionally close, making for a happy family unit. Home life was active and fun and there were outings and picnics, often embarked upon on a whim. The town itself was quaint, picture book pretty and safe. It was as you'd imagine a perfect life to be in rural America and it was all about to end.

At around 9 a.m. on the morning of Sunday, September 16, 1973, two Maine State Police detectives arrived at the Dill residence in West Gardiner. Robert and Janice Dill were asked to step outside so that the officers could speak privately with them. What they had to share was devastating. The body of a young woman had been found beside her car on Whippoorwill Road in nearby Litchfield, a location so remote that the locals called it Purgatory. The car was registered to the Dills' oldest daughter, Debbie, and the police needed them to come down to the morgue to identify her body.

Thus began a descent into hell for the Dill family. The body at the morgue was badly beaten, her facial features battered and bruised. Janice and Robert only recognized their 18-year-old daughter by a small scar on her forehead. Questioning the officers, Robert learned that his daughter's car had apparently run off the road and that she had then been attacked with a hammer, beaten so savagely on the head that there were holes punched through her skull. Debbie had never stood a chance, but she'd put up a fierce fight. Blood and skin cells were retrieved from under her fingernails. Since the body was found with its lower garments removed the suggestion was that this was a sexually motivated attack although the autopsy results would be inconclusive.

Robert and Janice Dill returned to their home that day broken. Still, there was a terrible duty to perform. They had to tell their children that Debbie was dead. That task fell to Robert, but he could not bring himself to utter the word 'murder' in reference to his oldest child. He told Debbie's siblings that she had died in a car accident. That family secret would prevail for the next seven years.

In the meantime, there was a homicide investigation to run, a brutal killer to be taken off the streets. The obvious place to start the inquiries was with those closest to the victim. According to the Dills, their daughter had recently become engaged to a young man named Kenneth Gillman, who happened to be a Lewiston police officer.

Brought in for questioning, Gillman said that he'd last seen Debbie when she left his apartment just before 1 a.m. Sunday morning. Debbie had brought along some wedding invitations to show him, and this had led to some tension between them. Ken had told her that she was moving too fast. He wasn't sure if he was ready to settle down just yet.

Might that have been a motive for murder? Had he and Debbie argued about their conflicting relationship goals? Gillman said no and he had the perfect alibi to back up his denials. He'd been working a shift and had attended to several verifiable complaints, including a domestic disturbance. That eliminated him as a person of interest.

The next suspect to emerge in the Debra Dill investigation came straight out of left field. Two days after the murder, on September 18, police received a report of a man 'behaving strangely' at a local restaurant. Taken into custody, the man continued his bizarre ranting, telling the officers that he had gotten into a fight with a man and had struck him with a hammer. Then he said that he'd argued with a woman wearing brown slacks. That caused the officers to sit up and take notice. Debra Dill had been killed with a hammer and had been wearing brown slacks at the time of her death. Had the police just lucked out in trapping their killer?

The answer to that question was no. The man did have a hammer, which the police found lying beside his car. That hammer had blood on it, but it was not Debra Dill's blood. The police had learned in the interim that the suspect was a former mental patient. His known movements at the time of Debbie's murder meant that he could not have killed her. Since they could not link him to any crime, he was free to go.

There would be one more serious suspect over the course of the investigation. His name was Frank White, and he was Debbie Dill's former boyfriend. By all accounts, he'd been upset by their breakup, madder still when he learned that she was engaged to be married. That, of course, gave him a strong motive but he also had an alibi. He'd been partying with friends on the night of the murder. At least six people could vouch for his whereabouts.

White was cut up over Debbie's death, certainly more affected than Ken Gillman. Two months after he was questioned by police, Frank White took his own life. Some in West Gardiner believed that he was driven to suicide by guilt. Others held that he could not deal with the death of the woman he still loved.

In any unsolved homicide, there comes a point where investigators can go no further. All of the leads have been run down, all of the suspects questioned and eliminated. The Dill case had been worked hard, generating a ton of paperwork that included over 400 recorded interviews. It had reached the point that all investigators dread. The trail had gone cold. It would remain so until 1986 when it landed on the desk of Detective Steven Drake, newly assigned to the Maine State Police's cold case division.

Eager to make his mark on a case that most considered unsolvable, Drake worked the clues hard, keeping at it for two years solid, going over every scrap of evidence. Then, in 1988, he got an unexpected break. It came via a telephone call from the Bridgeport Correction Center in Connecticut, where a prisoner had confessed to killing a man in a bar fight in Maine back in 1973.

The inmate who'd made this admission was a habitual criminal named Michael Boucher, a name that meant nothing to Drake at that time. And the confession that he'd made appeared false. Try as he might,

Drake could find no record of a fatal bar fight during the time frame mentioned. Then Drake started looking into Boucher's background. What he found, made him sit up and pay attention.

For starters, Boucher was a man with a long history of violence against women. Second, he was a native of Lewiston and had been living in the area at the time that Debbie Dill was murdered. Was it possible that he might have been involved? To test that theory, Drake tracked down one of Boucher's victims, a woman named Emily Campbell.

The attack on Emily Campbell had occurred in the early morning hours of June 4, 1974, nine months after Debbie Dill was bludgeoned to death. Emily had worked a late shift that night and was driving home when she was rear-ended by another vehicle. Thinking that it was an accident, she pulled over. The other vehicle then stopped behind her, with the driver remaining inside. Emily took a notepad out of her glove compartment and got out of her car so that she could write down the other driver's license plate number. She was doing that when the driver suddenly emerged, holding a length of steel pipe.

Emily was struck several times but managed to get back into her vehicle. She kicked at her attacker as he tried to drag her out and was able to fend him off while she got the passenger door open. Then she was out the other side and running before her attacker could round the vehicle to stop her. Fortunately, she could remember his license plate number and later passed it on to the police. She was also able to pick out Michael Boucher from a photo array.

This technique, called 'bump and run' by the police, is a common tactic employed by certain rapists. They deliberately drive into the vehicle of an intended victim, hoping they'll take it as an accident and pull over. Now Det. Drake had to wonder whether the same technique had been used on Debbie Dill. An examination of the crime scene photos confirmed that it had. There were noticeable impact marks on the rear bumper of Debbie's car. That confirmed the M.O. Now, Drake had to see if he could place Boucher at the scene.

And so, Det. Drake tracked down one of Michael Boucher's former wives, a woman named Anita. She was more than willing to cooperate and what she had to say was illuminating. In the early morning hours of September 16, 1973, Boucher had arrived home covered in blood, his hands cut and bruised. He claimed that he'd been involved in a fight and handed his bloody clothes to his wife, telling her to wash them right away. Later that morning he asked her to help him clean his car. While doing so, she discovered a hammer under the driver's seat. It was covered in red, rust-like stains and so she asked if she should wash it. Boucher said no. He was going to get rid of it.

Months later, Boucher would confess to his wife that he'd lied about the fight. He told her that he'd driven a woman off the road and beaten her to death. The woman, he claimed, had insulted him after they met in a donut shop. Anita wasn't sure if she believed him, but she knew what her husband was capable of. In fact, she was so terrified of Michael Boucher that she continued to keep his secret, even after they divorced.

This was explosive evidence. But Drake knew that he would need something to corroborate it, some means of linking Boucher to Debbie

Dill. And so, the detective obtained a warrant for Boucher's last known address. It was here, in the garage, that he found what he was looking for. The killer had kept trophies from the many women he'd victimized over the years. Among those was an invitation to an event that would never happen, the wedding invitation that Debbie had so excitedly shown to her fiancé on the night that she died.

Investigators now believed that they could piece together the last hours of Debbie Dill's life. After leaving Ken Gillman's apartment, the young woman had driven towards her parents' home in nearby West Gardiner. On the way there, she'd made the fateful decision to stop at a donut shop. She wanted to surprise her siblings with a treat at breakfast. It was at the donut shop that Michael Boucher spotted her. When Debbie drove away, he followed.

Whippoorwill Road was a familiar shortcut for Debbie but on this night, it played right into the hands of her pursuer. Had she taken the turnpike, he would never have had the opportunity to run her off the road. As it was, he hit her from behind, causing her to pull over. Then, as Boucher approached her vehicle, Debbie must have had a premonition of danger because she drove off again.

But that only served to anger Boucher. When he rear-ended Debbie for a second time, it was with enough force to send her vehicle careening off into the bushes. Boucher then approached, holding a hammer. He pulled Debbie kicking and screaming from the car and launched a frenzied attack, causing irreparable damage to her skull. Then, according to what he later told his wife, he raped her, inflicting the final indignity as she lay dying or already dead.

The Maine police were now confident that they had their man. However, it would take a laborious two-year process before Boucher was eventually extradited to stand trial. Court proceedings began in the summer of 1991 and resulted in a guilty verdict and a sentence of life in prison. The sentence, however, fell under the statute in place at the time of the murder. That meant that Boucher would be eligible for release in just ten years.

Michael Boucher has come up for parole five times. On each of those occasions, Debbie Dill's siblings have appeared before the board to oppose his application. They have vowed to continue the fight until Boucher eventually dies behind bars. Now in his seventies, Boucher remains in prison, serving his own form of purgatory.

Cookie Monster

In the neighborhood of Lakeland, Florida where she lived, Anna Houston was known as the 'Cookie Lady.' This was because she was a skilled baker and frequently treated the local children to her fresh-baked goods. Still sprightly and active at 79, Anna was a regular attendee at Lakeside Church of the Nazarene. She maintained a neat and orderly home at the government-subsidized Westlake housing project, where she did all her own housework. Her yard was likewise kept in tiptop condition, although here Anna frequently called on the local teens for help.

It was with this in mind that one of these youngsters arrived at Anna Houston's house on the afternoon of Monday, May 7, 1984. The young man was looking to earn a few bucks mowing the lawn and raking leaves but got no response when he rang the bell. He then circled around to the rear, where he found both the screen and back door standing ajar.

"Mrs. Houston?" he called out. No response. Easing the door open, the boy took a step into the kitchen. Then he stopped. For a moment, his brain couldn't quite register what he was seeing. Anna Houston was lying on the floor, dressed in a blue floral housecoat. Her face and hair and upper body were covered in blood. More of the stuff was pooled on the floor and spattered on the surrounding surfaces. Mrs. Houston's eyeglasses had been knocked from her face and were lying against a cabinet. A cutlery drawer stood open. The teen took in these details in the blink of an eye. Then he was turning and sprinting away, running for help.

Anna Houston's nearly eight-decade sojourn on this planet had not come to a peaceful end. The petite, 100-pound widow had been savagely knifed to death, with deep penetrating stab wounds to her neck, face, and chest. One of the knife thrusts had penetrated a lung. Another had opened a neck artery. There were slashes to the scalp that cut right to the bone. In addition, Anna's hands had suffered tendon-severing defensive wounds. She'd put up a valiant but futile fight.

The weapon that had inflicted these terrible wounds would never be found. However, detectives surmised that it had come from the victim's kitchen, hence the cutlery door that was found pulled out. It was also assumed that Anna might have known her killer since there was no evidence of forced entry to the home. Then again, the victim had been a trusting sort and not particularly security conscious. As for the motive behind this terrible crime, that remained a mystery. The house had not been ransacked and Anna had not been sexually assaulted. A personal motive also seemed unlikely. Everyone had loved the Cookie Lady.

There was one more important clue that would emerge from the crime scene. Back at the lab, forensic teams started working through the trace evidence and discovered that there were two distinct blood types in the samples they'd collected. The killer had cut himself, leaving his blood at the scene. That was of limited investigatory use back in the early 80s but would prove to be a case breaker in the future.

Detective Janet Franson had been a rookie patrol officer back when Anna Houston was murdered. She'd taken a keen interest in the case. The brutality meted out to such a frail old woman had repulsed her, instilling in her a determination to bring the perpetrator to justice. She'd been as frustrated as anyone as the leads dried up and the case went cold.

As months turned into years, though, Det. Franson found herself more determined than ever for a resolution. She made a pledge, as much to herself as to Anna Houston. She would not give up until the case was solved, the killer in custody. By the mid-90s, by now promoted to detective, Franson had not forgotten that promise. A considerable amount of her spare time was spent running down leads in the case. When the investigation was officially reopened in 1999, she was at the front of the queue, volunteering her expertise and enthusiasm.

Franson already knew the case pretty well, of course. She knew that there was very little in the files that hadn't been worked and reworked a dozen times. What was needed was fresh input. A murder in such a close-knit community could not have occurred without leaving some trace of itself. Someone must know something. Someone must have said something out of turn. Somewhere, there was a witness holding onto secrets.

It was with this in mind that Detective Franson approached a reporter from The Ledger newspaper in late 1999. Her hope was that a new story on the case might trigger someone's memory or conscience and bring them forward with information. That belief would be validated after the article appeared on the front page of The Ledger on January 4, 2000. It brought in a steady trickle of tips, several of them pointing to the same suspect, a man named Robert Austin Jr.

Austin was not exactly a stranger to law enforcement. When his name first appeared on police radars, the 31-year-old was serving a prison term for drug-related offenses. He also was not a stranger to Anna Houston. At the time of her death, he'd been living right next door to her, with his parents. Austin would have been just 15 at the time and he frequently did yardwork for Mrs. Houston, as well as enjoying the free cookies she handed out. That put him in the proximity of the crime scene but what possible motive could he have had for murdering his elderly neighbor?

According to the tipster – Robert Austin's former girlfriend, Sandra Chancey – it all came down to a squabble over money. Austin had been drinking that day and had decided to visit Mrs. Houston to ask for a few bucks. When the old woman refused, he became abusive. Anna demanded that he leave, threatening to call the police. Robert then started pushing her and things escalated quickly from there. At some point, he opened the cutlery drawer and took out a knife. He started stabbing Mrs. Houston, plunging the blade in again and again, until his victim lay dead on the floor. Then he fled the scene.

Austin had repeated this story many times to Sandra Chancey. He told her that he'd left the house covered in blood, some of it his own. He'd cut his hand during the struggle and even had a scar to prove it. And Sandra wasn't the only person to hear this confession from Austin. He'd also spoken about the murder to two of his friends. Neither of them had believed him at the time but they both came forward after reading the Ledger article.

It was time for investigators to have a chat with Robert Austin. They knew exactly where to find him. They arrived at the penitentiary on February 22, 2000, armed with a search warrant that compelled Austin to provide a blood sample for DNA comparison. That sample was subsequently sent to the lab, where it was tested against the blood found at the crime scene. It matched. After 16 years, Det. Franson had her man. Anna Houston's killer had been caught at last.

But Austin wasn't going down without a fight. At trial, defense attorney Robert Gray raised some compelling reasonable doubt arguments. The first of these was that Austin had been inside the Houston residence on several occasions and that it was therefore no surprise that his DNA was found at the scene. The second was to offer an alternate suspect, a former neighbor of Anna Houston, now deceased. According to Gray, it was this individual who was the killer. He supported this assertion by suggesting that Mrs. Houston had been killed during a sexual assault.

Unfortunately for Gray, neither of his arguments held up under scrutiny. There was zero evidence that a sexual assault had taken place. Gray's claim that semen had been retrieved from the victim's body was blown out of the water when an agent of the Florida Department of Law Enforcement took the stand and testified that this was not the case. A vaginal swab had been performed but had turned up no trace of seminal fluid.

Gray's argument that the presence of Austin's DNA could have an innocent explanation was similarly flawed. Had the DNA been lifted from a surface area or a light switch or drinking glass, then the logic might have worked. But this was DNA found in blood, blood that had been retrieved from a victim who'd been viciously knifed to death. There was only one way that it could have gotten there. Austin had cut himself during the act. He still had that scar that he liked to show off while boasting about savaging an elderly woman.

Robert Austin Jr. was convicted of first-degree murder and sentenced to life in prison. A self-inflicted wound and an extremely persistent detective had brought him to justice. But for that, he would have gotten away with murder.

Snapshots from Hell

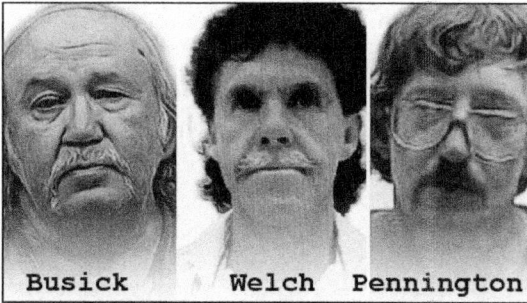

Busick   Welch   Pennington

Ashley Freeman and Lauria Bible had known each other since kindergarten. The girls were fast friends, almost like sisters, so when Ashley celebrated her 16th birthday on December 29, 1999, it was no surprise who she wanted to spend the day with. That day would include dinner at a pizza restaurant in their hometown of Welch, Oklahoma, just south of the Kansas state line. Thereafter, the friends went back to Ashley's house, where Lauria would be spending the night.

At around 5:30 a.m. the next morning, a Craig County 911 dispatcher received a call about a mobile home ablaze on the outskirts of Welch, billowing black smoke into the sky. Firefighters were immediately dispatched to the scene, but they could do very little to save the home, which was all but gutted by the time they arrived. All they could do was quell the flames and pray that there was no one trapped inside. That would turn out to be a vain hope. The severely burned body of 37-year-old Kathy Freeman was found lying on the floor of her destroyed bedroom.

Right from the start, it was clear that this was no accident. The fire had its source in a wood-burning stove and it was obvious to investigators that an accelerant had been used to spread the blaze. The autopsy on Kathy Freeman would also reveal that Kathy had not succumbed to the flames but had been shot in the head. The fire had been a device to cover up the murder and that suggested a clear suspect. Danny Freeman was missing along with his teenage daughter, Ashley.

And, as investigators were about to learn, Ashley wasn't the only teen who'd been in the house that night. The car that they found parked in the drive was registered to Ashley's best friend, Lauria Bible. The working theory at this stage was that Danny Freeman had killed his wife and started the fire before abducting the girls and fleeing the scene. A statewide bulletin was therefore issued, and a search initiated.

However, the police and fire crews had both missed something crucial at the burned-out house. Danny Freeman wasn't missing. Danny Freeman was dead. His charred remains were hidden in the twisted wreckage of the trailer. It was Lauria Bible's parents, Jay and Lorene, who found him, while they were searching for clues to their daughter's whereabouts. Thereafter, search teams returned to the house and went over the site again, more carefully this time. They found no trace of the missing girls. Ashley and Lauria had vanished.

What had happened to the girls? Perhaps the most popular theory, fueled by local rumor, was that Danny and Kathy Freeman had owed money to local drug dealers and had been killed when they were unable to pay. The girls had likely been dragged away to be raped and murdered or perhaps sold into sex slavery.

An alternate notion was that the murders were connected to another tragedy that had happened earlier that same year. The Freemans' teenage son, Shane, had been shot and killed by a local deputy while trying to steal a car. The shooting had been ruled 'justified' but the Freemans had threatened a lawsuit and had been at war with the Craig County Sherriff's Department ever since. Now, the rumor mill was awash with allegations that the cops had murdered the family to make the problem go away.

There wasn't a shred of proof to back up these accusations. Still, Deputy David Hayes, the officer involved in the shooting, was asked to take a polygraph. Hayes passed but that did nothing to make the rumors go away. The Craig County police were under scrutiny and even more determined than usual to close the case, if only to clear their name.

With the Oklahoma State Bureau of Investigation (OSBI) also involved, no stone was left unturned in the search for the missing girls. Divers were sent to the depths of Grand Lake and to a water-filled quarry near Chelsea. Officers rappelled into a disused mine shaft near Picher. The house of a habitual sex offender was searched after a jailhouse tip-off. A field was excavated after the discovery of some bones, which turned out to be of animal origin. The case was featured on 'America's Most Wanted.' Reported sightings took investigators as far afield as California, Mexico, and Canada. None of these efforts bore fruit.

The Freeman/Bible case would also gain notoriety due to the involvement of two notorious serial killers. In May of 2002, Texas death row inmate Tommy Lee Sells, known as the 'Coast to Coast Killer,' claimed that he was responsible for the deaths. However, Sells' confession did not tie up with the actual crimes and was soon dismissed. He would later admit that he'd just wanted a few days out of his cell, leading the authorities on a wild goose chase to non-existent dumpsites.

Jeremy Bryan Jones was somewhat more convincing. The rapist and killer of at least eight women, Jones entered the conversation in 2005, when he claimed that he was the man who'd killed Ashley and Lauria. According to Jones, he'd killed the adults as a favor to a drug dealer and had abducted, raped, and murdered the girls. Jones claimed that he'd tossed their bodies into a mine shaft in Galena, Kansas. When a search turned up nothing, Jones recanted, saying that he'd made the whole thing up to gain food and phone privileges.

The Jones 'confession' would be the last significant action in the investigation for over a decade. Thereafter, the case when cold, with very little possibility that it would ever be solved. Any forensic evidence had gone up in flames and there were no witnesses, at least none who were prepared to come forward.

But the police did have one important clue, even if they failed to recognize its significance at the time. In the days following the murders, an insurance card was found near the crime scene. It belonged to a young woman who was questioned but swore that she did not know how the card had ended up there. The police left it at that but perhaps they should have dug a little deeper. The woman in question was dating a local ne'er-do-good at that time, a man named Warren Phillip Welch, Phil to his friends and customers.

Phil was a man of uneven temperament, quick to anger and keen to use his fists when annoyed. Most often, those fists were employed against the women in his life and Phil had served time for domestic violence and for making a terrorist threat. It was also well-known in Craig County that Phil Welch was a methamphetamine cook and drug dealer. When not involved in the manufacture and sale of narcotics, he was a student of the 'Good Book' and was known to sprout long passages from the scriptures.

Phil Welch frequently hung out with two associates of equally questionable character, David Pennington and Ronnie Busick. Given the rumors doing the rounds at the time of the murders, that Danny Freeman was a drug dealer and that he'd been killed over an unpaid debt, this trio of miscreants should have been of obvious interest to the police. Somehow, they slipped through the cracks and were never seriously considered as suspects.

There was another piece of intelligence that flew under the radar of law enforcement during the fallow years of the investigation. It had to do with a rumor about a macabre set of Polaroids. If the stories were to be believed, these were in the possession of Phil Welch, who supposedly kept them in a leather briefcase in his trailer. These pictures have never been found although several witnesses have come forward claiming to have seen them. They were photographs of Ashley Freeman and Lauria Bible, trussed and gagged on a bed. Some of the shots apparently feature Phil Welch, lying beside his clearly terrified victims, a grin on his face.

By the time the authorities eventually learned of these photographs, both Welch and Pennington were dead. Welch had passed in 2007; Pennington in 2015. That left only Ronnie Busick to answer for the crimes and Busick had long since quit town. He was eventually tracked to Wichita, Kansas, and extradited to Oklahoma in April 2018. By now 66 years old, morbidly obese, and walking with the use of a cane, Busick initially denied any involvement in the murders. However, he eventually admitted to being an accessory. It was Phil Welch, he claimed, who'd killed the Freemans and Lauria Bible.

According to Busick, he and Welch and Pennington had arrived at the Freemans' trailer that night, to collect on an outstanding drug debt. Danny Freeman was overdue on a payment of $2,800, for two ounces of meth that he'd purchased from Welch. But Freeman couldn't pay, and an argument ensued during which Freeman went for a gun he had sitting on the table. That was a mistake. Welch was carrying a sawn-off shotgun in his coat and blasted Freeman. Then, deciding that he didn't want to leave any witnesses behind, he also killed Kathy Freeman.

The girls, meanwhile, had heard the gunshots and escaped through a window. They were hiding in the field while the men ransacked the trailer and then set it alight. Had they kept their heads down, they would likely have escaped. Unfortunately, they stood up to see what was going on and were spotted. They were chased down and caught, dragged to Welch's truck, and then driven 15 miles over rural roads to Welch's trailer in the neighboring town of Picher. They would be held here over several terrifying days, during which they were repeatedly raped and subjected to torture. Eventually, Welch grew tired of having them around and strangled them.

This confession was a terrible thing for the families of the victims to hear. But at least it presented the hope that the location of their loved one's remains would be revealed, so that they could be retrieved for burial. Unfortunately, this was not to be. According to Busick, he did not accompany Welch and Pennington when they went to dispose of the bodies. All he knows is that they were thrown into a pit.

Ronnie Busick entered a guilty plea to accessory to first-degree murder in July 2020. He was sentenced to 15 years in prison. Afflicted with type 2 diabetes, lung disease, and with several tumors growing on his spine, he is very likely to die behind bars. Ashley Freeman and Lauria Bible have never been found. Neither have the Polaroids, those snapshots from hell depicting their terrifying last days.

Double Trouble

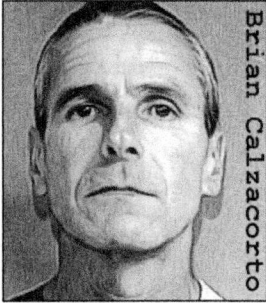

Brian Calzacorto

Laurie Colannino was the kind of woman who turned heads. Beautiful, vivacious, fun, outgoing, these were words that were frequently applied to the 23-year-old cocktail waitress from Clearwater, Florida. But Laurie was more than just a pretty face. This was a young woman with ambitions. Typical of her, those ambitions involved helping others. In December 1990, Laurie applied to paramedic school. It was her dream to qualify as an EMT.

On the afternoon of January 2, 1990, Laurie Colannino returned from a workout at the gym. The Bay Pointe Apartments where she lived, is a sprawling complex of 52 detached buildings, each of them comprising eight units. Laurie entered hers at around 1 p.m., leaving her door open so that her cat could go out. She then picked up the phone and dialed her friend, Scott Kelly. Scott had worked a late shift as a barman and was asleep when his phone rang. The pair started talking but then Laurie suddenly let out a gasp and the phone went dead. Concerned, Scott immediately called back. All he got was Laurie's answering machine. It would take several tries before Laurie eventually picked up. "Everything's okay," she told him. "I've got to go." Then the phone was dead again.

But everything was clearly not okay. Throwing on some clothes, Scott ran down to his car and started driving to Laurie's apartment. He arrived to find the door standing ajar. It was in the bedroom that he found his friend, lying on the floor, dressed only in a bloodstained t-shirt and a pair of gym socks. Scott immediately fell to his knees beside Laurie and started CPR. But it was soon clear that it was too late. Laurie was beyond help. Staggering to his feet, Scott went to the phone and dialed 911.

To the detectives who arrived on the scene, the motive for this terrible crime was easy to determine. Semen on the dead woman's thighs was a giveaway. But whoever had done this, also appeared to harbor a great deal of resentment towards the victim. Laurie had been stabbed multiple times. The autopsy would count 16 deep wounds, all of them centered on a small area around the heart. This overkill suggested a personal motive and right now the police had a good suspect standing right in front of them.

Laurie and Scott Kelly had been more than just friends and work colleagues. Turns out, they'd had an on-again-off-again sexual relationship, kind of a "friends with benefits" thing. Such relationships, although casual in principle, can often lead to festering jealousies. Is that what had happened here? Scott said no and insisted that he'd loved Laurie as a friend. He readily agreed to provide a blood sample for DNA analysis. Back then, the lab work could take months. For now, the police had no reason to detain Scott Kelly. He was free to go.

But, as investigators were about to learn, Laurie Colannino had a rather convoluted love life. She was currently dating a chef named Eric Held and had an ex-boyfriend named Wayne Le Fleur, who she'd recently reported for stalking her and for vandalizing her car. Both men were brought in and questioned, and both offered alibis and agreed to provide blood samples. It would be a long wait before DNA could either clear them or flag one of them as a killer.

Not that the police were placing all of their faith in DNA. Officers descended on the Bay Pointe Apartments and started questioning residents. This was a massive undertaking but ultimately it would come up empty. Despite a vicious murder committed in a densely populated commune, no one had seen or heard anything. Months passed without a break. Then the DNA results were back, clearing all of the original suspects. With detectives thinly stretched and dealing with several other homicides, including an ongoing serial killer case, the Laurie Colannino inquiry was quietly shelved. It would remain stagnant until 1994.

That was when the Pinellas County Cold Case unit decided to take another look at the evidence. Technology had moved on in the intervening years. DNA tests were now faster and less expensive. It allowed the investigative team to undertake an ambitious project, testing every adult male who'd been living in the complex at the time of the murder. A surprisingly high number of these individuals still called the Bay Pointe home and most of them agreed to provide a blood sample.

All but one, in fact. The police were having a hard time tracking down Brian Calzacorto, a 31-year-old shoe salesman who lived in eyeshot of

Laurie's former residence. Detectives made several visits to
Calzacorto's apartment but never found him at home. Notes were left,
asking him to get in touch. Each time, Calzacorto failed to respond.
That made him a person of interest, worthy of further examination.
What investigators learned next only deepened their suspicions.

It turned out that Calzacorto was a suspect in another murder, the 1986
shooting death of his father, a police officer in his hometown of
Donora, Pennsylvania. A Grand Jury had been convened in that case,
but it had been torpedoed by the extended Calzacorto family. Each and
every one of them had taken the Fifth on the stand, refusing to answer
even the most mundane of questions. Even Calzacorto's widowed
mother refused to speak up against the son who'd likely murdered her
husband. As a result, the D.A. did not get the indictment he wanted.
Brian Calzacorto had moved to Florida, where he'd taken up residence
at the Bay Pointe Apartments. Now, he was embroiled in another
murder.

The police were desperate to speak to Brian Calzacorto. It would be
weeks before they caught a break in tracking him down. That was
when Calzacorto's brother, Alfred, called in and reported him missing.
According to Alfred, he'd been unable to reach Brian for several days.
Using this as cover, detectives agreed to meet Alfred at his brother's
apartment. They were stunned when they saw him. Alfred was a
deadringer for their suspect. The two of them were identical twins.

And that presented investigators with a unique opportunity. Since
identical twins have the same DNA profile, they could test Alfred
against their crime scene evidence. If they got a match, they'd know
that Brian was their man. The problem was that Alfred was wise to

this. He had stood by his brother when he was accused of murdering their father and he had his back again now. He refused point blank to provide a blood sample.

Tracking down Brian Calzacorto was now the primary focus of the investigation. But Calzacorto appeared to have abandoned his apartment and he'd also absconded from his job. Investigators weren't even sure that he was still in Florida. Seven weeks passed before the police got another break. Calzacorto was arrested for theft after he was caught pickpocketing on Clearwater Beach. He'd soon find himself under interrogation for a far more serious crime.

But Calzacorto was giving nothing away. Cool and collected under interrogation, he denied knowing Laurie Colannino and claimed that he'd been at work when she was killed. He also refused to provide a blood sample. Without probable cause to obtain a court order, the police had to let it drop. Despite their strong belief that Calzacorto was their man, they were forced to watch him walk away. He would remain at liberty for the next five years.

By 2001, Laurie Colannino had been dead for eleven years. Her mother had died in the interim, never knowing who had stolen the life of her beloved daughter, never seeing justice done. The Pinellas County police, meanwhile, were as determined as ever to take down the killer. They'd kept tabs on Calzacorto over the years, watched as he moved to Tampa, set up an apartment, and got a job at another shoe store. DNA technology had also made advancements during this time. It was no longer necessary to take a blood sample from a suspect. A profile could now be extracted from any biological material.

Criminal cases are often resolved by the most mundane of actions. In the case of Brian Calzacorto, it was the act of taking out the trash. One night in 2001, Calzacorto walked out of his apartment and dumped a trash bag into an outside bin. He then walked back into his building, never knowing that he was being surveilled. The minute he was out of sight, officers emerged to retrieve the bag. It delivered a treasure trove of potential evidence, including a razor from which skin cells were extracted. Subjected to DNA analysis, it provided a perfect match to the semen found at the crime scene.

That should have made this an open-and-shut case. But there was one major complication for prosecutors to overcome. Twins have identical DNA. How could they prove that it was Brian and not Alfred who had raped and killed Laurie Colannino? The defense, of course, was already thinking along these lines. In fact, it is quite likely that Alfred was on board with the strategy. Although he denied on the stand that he had killed Laurie, he did not appear particularly affronted by being accused of murder. It was left to the jury to draw its own conclusions

In the end, it came down to proximity. Alfred had been working in Tampa at that time, in a secure building that required him to sign in and out. He'd just started the job, which meant that he would not have had time off. Given the 30-minute drive he'd have to make either way, it would have been impossible for him to commit the murder. Brian, on the other hand, worked just a short walk from his residence at the Bay Pointe Apartments. He'd have had no problem committing the murder and then returning to work. His semen at the crime scene proved that he had done exactly that.

The prosecution argued that Calzacorto had been standing in his apartment when he spotted Laurie Colannino returning from the gym. He'd probably seen her before, perhaps at the complex swimming pool where she enjoyed lounging. Laurie was a woman who easily attracted male attention. Calzacorto had probably been lusting after her for some time. On this day, he decided to act on his desires.

Picking up a knife, he crossed the short distance from his building to hers. Laurie was on the phone when he entered her apartment, but Calzacorto cut the call off. Then, after Scott King tried calling her back, Calzacorto forced her to call him and say that everything was okay. He then dragged the terrified woman into her bedroom and raped her. Finally, after sating his lust, he plunged the knife into her chest, then repeated the action again and again. Laurie tried fighting back, sustaining defensive wounds to her hands in the process. But she was no match for the man straddling her, pinning her down, wielding the blade with deadly purpose. The police had initially theorized that the overkill of the crime suggested a personal motive. They did not consider that the killer might be a bloodthirsty psychopath, who got off on the pain and terror he inflicted.

One of the real tragedies of this case is that Brian Calzacorto should never have been free to harm Laurie Colannino or any other woman. Had his family not closed ranks after the murder of Alfred Calzacorto Sr., then Brian would probably have been locked away and Laurie Colannino would still be with her loved ones, perhaps a qualified paramedic, perhaps raising a family of her own. Too late, the courts were able to deliver justice to a heartless killer. Brian Calzacorto was sentenced to life in prison, with no parole for 25 years.

The Killer Upstairs

It was the evening of August 2, 1991, and in Dallas, Texas, Felicia Prechtl was planning a rare night out. The 29-year-old single mom was devoted to her five-year-old son, Shad, but just for tonight, she'd arranged for her brother and his girlfriend to babysit the boy while she went out with friends. Shad, in any case, was excited to spend time with his Uncle Michael, especially when Michael announced a trip to the store to pick up some videos and snacks for the evening. It was around six when Michael, Shad, and Michael's girlfriend departed on their store run. Felicia stayed behind to finish her hair and makeup for her night on the town. She was thus engaged when there was a knock on the door.

Felicia vaguely recognized the man standing in the hall. She'd seen him around the apartment complex. Now, he introduced himself, saying that his name was Karl and that he lived upstairs from her. "I was wondering if I could borrow some sugar," he said, timidly holding out a cup. Felicia, of course, said that he could and invited him inside. After filling his cup, she sent him on his way and got back to doing her makeup. But just a couple of minutes later, there was another knock. Setting aside a tube of mascara, Felicia went to answer it. Looking through the peephole, she was somewhat surprised to see that Karl was back.

A short while later, Michael and Shad returned from the store. Shad was keen to show his mom the videos they'd rented but Felicia was in the bathroom with the door shut, the clothes she'd picked out for the evening hanging in the hall. Shad and his babysitters went to sit in the lounge but after several minutes Michael began to become concerned about his sister. He went to the bathroom door and knocked, calling her name. No reply came from within. He tried again. Nothing. Slowly, Michael eased the door open, warning his sister that he was coming in. "I hope you're decent," he joked. Then he saw what was inside and the words died on his lips.

Felicia was lying face down on the bathroom floor, her jeans and underwear pulled down to her knees, her wrists and ankles bound with duct tape. A pool of blood was haloed out around her head, deep crimson against the white of the tile. Michael did not have to check for a pulse to know that there was nothing to be done. Shaken, stunned, barely able to comprehend what had happened here, he pulled the door shut. Then he walked to the bedroom and called the police.

Felicia Prechtl had been executed by a single .30 caliber bullet to the head, fired on a trajectory that suggested she'd either been kneeling on the floor or sitting on the toilet when she was killed. Before that, she had been bound hand and foot and brutally sodomized. But the killer had been far from careful. He'd left behind a .30 caliber cartridge; he'd left a fingerprint on the duct tape he'd used on Felicia's wrists; he'd left semen on his victim. Given that this was a murder committed inside a heavily trafficked area and within a defined window of time;

given that it had been reported almost immediately; this looked like a very solvable case.

However, as detectives started questioning residents of the building, they hit their first roadblock. No one had seen or heard anything. Karl was questioned, of course, but insisted that he'd been out walking his dogs. This was confirmed by a neighbor. Karl made no mention of the cup of sugar he'd borrowed from the victim that very evening. Next, the police turned to their forensic evidence. A DNA profile was extracted from the seminal fluid and submitted to CODIS. No match. The fingerprint was run through the usual state and national databases. Nothing. In no time at all, the solvable case had run aground.

Five years passed. In early July 1996, a man named Karl Chamberlain was arrested for an attempted robbery and abduction in Houston. Chamberlain was booked on the charge and, of course, he was fingerprinted. The minute those prints were entered into the system, they returned a match, to the unsolved 1991 homicide of Felicia Prechtl. Dallas PD detectives were stunned when they got the news. A quick review of the case file told them that Chamberlain had been a neighbor of Felicia and had been questioned during the original inquiry. That put him in the vicinity of the murder. Not just in the vicinity, but at the scene, binding the victim's wrists with duct tape.

Karl Chamberlain was quickly tracked to the Dallas suburb of Euless and taken into custody on July 17, 1996. Questioned by detectives, he seemed almost eager to confess, although his version of events was dubious at best. According to Chamberlain, he'd been drinking heavily that day and decided to visit his attractive neighbor on the pretense of borrowing a cup of sugar. He said that Felicia was scantily dressed when she answered the door and claimed that she had flirted with him as she gave him the sugar. He then went back to his apartment but was sexually aroused by the encounter and decided to return. When he did so, he was carrying an M1 rifle and a roll of duct tape.

Chamberlain never could explain why he armed himself before he returned to Felicia's apartment. If it was to coerce her into having sex, that proved unnecessary. According to Chamberlain, Felicia consented to have anal intercourse. However, once the act was done, she started threatening to tell his wife and that was when he took the gun and shot her. Immediately afterward, he returned to his apartment and took his dogs for a walk, to establish an alibi.

Police detectives deal with the very best liars in the business. It goes with the territory. Over time, they develop near super-human abilities for sniffing out untruths. In effect, they are human polygraph machines. But you didn't need any advanced skills to realize that Karl Chamberlain was lying through his teeth. Were the police really to believe that a young woman preparing for a night out, and expecting her five-year-old son home at any time, would consent to anal sex with a stranger who just showed up at her door? The story was just too ludicrous to warrant serious consideration.

The far more likely course of events was that Chamberlain's sugar ruse was a scouting mission to establish whether Felicia was alone. Having determined that she was, he returned to his apartment to fetch the gun and duct tape, which he used to threaten and then bind his victim. Having done that, he sodomized her and then shot her in the head. That made sense. That matched the evidence, not the tall tale Chamberlain was telling.

Karl Eugene Chamberlain was indicted on capital murder charges in August 1996. In June 1997, he was found guilty as charged and sentenced to death. Of course, there was still the protracted appeals process to navigate. In Chamberlain's case that would take eleven years before he eventually kept his date with the executioner on June 11, 2008.

Chamberlain appeared in good spirits as he was strapped to the gurney, smiling broadly as he addressed Felicia Prechtl's relatives and told them that he loved them. "We are here to honor the life of Felecia Prechtl," he said, "and to celebrate my death. I wish I could die more than once to tell you how sorry I am." He then admonished them not to have hate in their hearts, his words fading away in mid-sentence as the drugs took effect.

Outside the prison gates, Chamberlain's supporters were in less conciliatory mood. A group of 20 anti-capital punishment campaigners had gathered and were loudly protesting the execution, with Chamberlain's mother to the fore. Mu'ina Arthur had traveled from Las Vegas, New Mexico to participate in the protest. "America is a fascist country," she shouted into a bullhorn. "My son is a jewel! He's a teddy bear! He is not a bad man!" Felicia Prechtl's family might have held a different opinion.

Late Night Caller

Back in the early 70s, Buffalo, New York, was a boomtown. A center for steel manufacture, with the mills running at full production, it was a magnet for laborers from across the country. There were jobs aplenty, money to be made. The steelworkers worked hard, and they played hard after hours. In the Riverside area of the city, where many of these men lived, there was a bar on every corner. They did a roaring trade every night of the week.

It is in the midst of this thriving community that we find Galen and Barbara Lloyd. Galen, known to friends and colleagues as Shorty, was a mill worker. His wife, Barbara, took care of the home and minded their two young children, Joseph, 3, and Kimberly, just 14 months old. This, however, was not a harmonious union. Shorty was a boozer who usually hit the bars directly from work. Barbara, although a good mother to her children, also liked to party and, if local gossip was to be believed, she was liberal with her sexual favors. It all meant that the couple was frequently at each other's throats. Neighbors often heard raised voices and angry shouts coming from their apartment.

On the evening of March 14, 1974, Shorty Lloyd left his job at the mill and followed a familiar path to one of his favorite watering holes. Shorty had a good excuse for needing a drink that night. He and his supervisor had exchanged words, and Shorty was convinced that the man was planning to fire him. In any case, Shorty hit the bottle hard, harder than even was the norm for him. He would visit eleven different drinking establishments that night, all of them within a short walk of his residence. Eventually, at four in the morning, he staggered home.

But Shorty had trouble getting into the house. He couldn't find his key and banging on the front door, shouting Barbara's name, brought no response from within. Eventually, he rounded the building. This brought him closer to the bedroom, so he hoped that he'd be able to rouse Barbara from here. As it turned out, there was no need. The back door stood open.

Under normal circumstances, this would have surprised Shorty. Barbara always made a big deal of locking the door at night, latching it from the inside. But Shorty's mind was muddled by booze. It did not even register with him that every light in the house was on. He staggered towards his bedroom, stopping briefly on the way to look in on his children. Joe and Kim were both sound asleep. Then Shorty continued down the hall, stopping in the doorway of his room. The bed that he shared with his wife was empty, the bedclothes piled on the floor. 'Barbara?" he slurred. That was when he spotted it, a pale hand protruding from under the comforter.

It was at this point that Shorty's inebriated brain registered that something was amiss. Stepping forward, he grabbed a corner of the comforter and peeled it back. A jolt of adrenalin rushed through him, banishing the cobwebs from his mind in an instant. Barbara lay on the floor, her eyes staring blankly towards the ceiling, her upper body covered in blood. From the center of her chest, protruded the handle of a knife. Shorty ran then, ran to his neighbor, Bob Innes, and pounded on his door until Bob opened. "Call the police!" he blurted. "It's Barb! Someone killed Barb!"

This was an incredibly savage murder. Barbara Lloyd had been butchered, stabbed 16 times in the upper body with a steak knife taken from her own kitchen. This had been wielded with such force that the blade had snapped off during the attack. Barbara had also been strangled, and the autopsy would reveal that she had been raped. Valuable forensic evidence was retrieved from the scene, including three pubic hairs found on the floor between the dead woman's legs.

Right from the start, the police were certain of one thing. The person who'd killed Barbara Lloyd was not a stranger to her. The fury of the attack suggested someone with a deep-seated anger. The fact that Barbara's face had been covered, implied that the killer could not bear to look at her after the deed was done. Whoever had killed Barbara was someone she knew, someone with whom she'd perhaps had a love/hate relationship.

And who did that describe almost exactly? Galen Lloyd, of course. There can be little doubt that Shorty loved his wife. In fact, his prodigious alcohol consumption might have had something to do with her serial infidelity. Was it a stretch to believe that Shorty came home drunk, that he and Barbara got into another of their rows, and that he lost his temper and killed her? No, that was not a stretch at all.

Shorty would spend over 12 hours under police interrogation. During that time, he made some telling admissions. He admitted, for example, that he had almost killed Barbara the week before she died. According to Shorty, Barbara had gone out that night while he took care of the kids. He had dozed off and woken at 5:30, only to find that she was not yet home. He'd then gone to the window and looked out into the street where he spotted Barbara sitting in a parked car with his neighbor, Bob Innes. He'd gone out and dragged her inside. Then the two of them got into it and he put his hands on her throat, choking her until she blacked out. "I thought I'd killed her," he told the cops. Now they wondered if Shorty might have gone one step further.

Speculation, however, has never closed a murder inquiry. In truth, the cops had nothing on Shorty. Detectives had verified his alibi. Shorty was well-known in the area and had been seen drinking all night at various bars. It wasn't a perfect alibi by a long shot, but it checked out. Shorty was free to go. Distraught at his wife's death, he sought solace in an old friend, the whiskey bottle. With their mother gone and their father in no condition to care for them, the children were sent to live with Barbara's sister, Linda, and her husband, Leon "Rusty" Chatt.

Rusty was an interesting character, one of the few men in the area who did not work in the steel industry. In fact, Rusty worked barely at all. He was a slacker, perpetually unemployed, usually scrounging for booze or money. He was also a ladies' man with a string of conquests around town. And if Rusty's charms failed to impress the object of his desire, then he was not averse to applying a bit of physical pressure. One of the women who'd attracted his unwanted attention was his sister-in-law, Barbara Lloyd. Barbara had confided in her friends that Rusty had once tried to force himself on her. When she resisted, he got physical and ended up ripping her blouse. According to those who knew Barbara, she was afraid of Rusty.

And so, Rusty was added to the list of suspects. Officers started talking to his drinking buddies and heard the same story time and again. It appeared that Rusty was obsessed with Barbara and that he often spoke about wanting to have sex with her. It was time to bring Rusty in for a talk.

Rusty Chatt's alibi for the night of the murder sounded a lot like the one provided by Shorty Lloyd. He too had been out partying, visiting many of the same bars. He and Shorty had spent some time together in the latter part of the evening. Rusty had even taken Shorty to the home of one of his girlfriends, a woman named Darnell. Shorty had left him there and gone back to his binge. Rusty had spent the rest of the night. Darnell, he said, would confirm it.

And Darnell did back up Rusty's story, adding one detail that was of particular interest to investigators. She said that Rusty had fresh scratches on his back that night. This was one of two snippets of information that began to swing suspicion in the direction of Rusty

Chatt. The other was Rusty's attire on the night in question. Early in the evening, several witnesses reported that he'd been wearing a blue shirt with a floral pattern. By the time he hooked up with Shorty, he was wearing a white t-shirt. Why had he changed?

That was an interesting question, but it did not amount to evidence of murder. Six months in and the police still did not have enough to charge either of their main suspects. The case was going nowhere. Rusty and his wife had left the area by then, and the children had been returned to the custody of their father. But Shorty continued to sink deeper and deeper into the bottle. Eventually, he lost his job and his children, who were placed in foster care. Meanwhile, the murder of Barbara Lloyd faded from the public consciousness. There seemed very little prospect that her killer would ever be caught.

By 2003, Barbara Lloyd had been dead 29 years and her case had been cold for almost that long. Her son Joe was now 32 years old; her daughter Kim was 30. Still haunted by their mother's death, still desperate for answers, the siblings approached the Buffalo Police Department to ask if they'd reopen the investigation. Buffalo did not have a cold case squad at that time, but they agreed, assigning Detective Dennis Delano to the task. The first challenge for Delano was to find the case file, which was buried deep in the archives. That task would take him four whole days.

Once the files were located, though, Delano learned that there were two main suspects, Galen 'Shorty' Lloyd, and Leon 'Rusty' Chatt. There was also a biological sample lifted from the scene, in the form of three pubic hairs. The obvious next step was to extract a DNA profile from the hairs and compare it against the suspects. That might implicate one of them or it might clear both.

Shorty Lloyd still lived in Buffalo and agreed immediately to provide a sample for testing. All these years he'd lived under the shadow of suspicion, with even his children wondering if he'd murdered their mother. This was his chance at absolution and Shorty took it with both hands. The DNA test cleared him.

That left Rusty Chatt who had long since left the area and was far more difficult to track. Investigators learned that Chatt was now divorced from his wife, had lived in several southern states, and had served five years in Arizona for robbery. Then he dropped off the radar for a while before reappearing in Buffalo in the late 1990s. When detectives eventually tracked him down, he was living in a rooming house less than a mile from the apartment in which Barbara Lloyd had been murdered.

It must have been a considerable shock to Rusty when Buffalo PD detectives knocked on his door, asking about a decades-old murder. Rusty said that he knew nothing about it and refused to submit to a DNA test. Then he closed the door in the officers' faces.

But Rusty should have known that the cops were not going to give up that easily. For weeks, they tracked him until Rusty made the ill-advised move of hawking up a wad of phlegm on an icy sidewalk. That was scooped up into an evidence vial and sent to the lab for testing. It would be two months before the results were in. The next time that Buffalo PD knocked on Rusty's door, it was with an arrest warrant.

Rusty Lloyd, of course, had an obvious defense. At trial, his attorney offered the thesis that Rusty had consensual sex with Barbara on the night she died, but that he was not her killer. That, attorney Joseph Terranova suggested, could only be one man, her husband, Galen Lloyd. The argument was enough to convince one holdout juror, resulting in a mistrial.

Second time around, the prosecution case was more persuasively presented. According to the prosecutor, Chatt had spotted Galen Lloyd drinking in the bar that night. Realizing that Barbara would be home alone, he'd gone to her house, determined to take what he'd lusted after for so long. He'd strangled Barbara into submission and raped her. Then, to cover up the rape, he'd stabbed her to death. Barbara had scratched him during the assault and those scratches would later be noticed by Chatt's girlfriend. He'd also gotten blood on his shirt which was why he'd changed it. Finally, he'd sought out his brother-in-law, Shorty, and spent the next few hours drinking with him, to establish an alibi.

Barbara Lloyd had turned down Rusty Chatt before, the prosecutor stated in summation, so why on the night she was murdered would she suddenly consent to have sex with him? The simple answer was that she hadn't agreed. Chatt had forced her and then killed her to ensure her silence. It was the only explanation that made sense.

March 14, 2008, marked 34 years to the day since Barbara Lloyd's murder. It was also the day that the jury returned a unanimous guilty verdict to the charge of second-degree murder. Rusty Chatt was subsequently sentenced to 25 years to life. Chatt was 67 years old on the day he entered prison. He will likely die behind bars.

Long Road to Justice

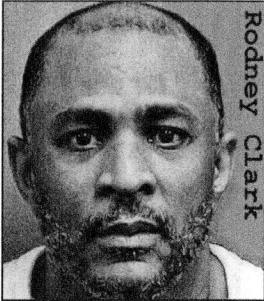

Dana Fader had been through some tough times in her life. The 27-year-old mother of three had seen her marriage fail and her children separated. She'd seen her ex move out of state with her oldest, a 10-year-old named Angela. She'd also had to place her middle child, Kolby, in the care of her parents. The two jobs she worked simply didn't foot the bills, especially when she had to constantly chase her former husband for child support for the youngest, Johnny. The little boy lived with Dana in an apartment in Lake Worth, Florida, a residence she shared with her brother, Joseph Bailey.

But at least Dana had a support system close at hand. Her mother and stepfather lived in the same building and her sister, Martha, was just down the hall. The siblings were close, so when Dana was feeling down, on the evening of June 19, 1987, after yet another fight with her ex, Martha suggested a girls' night out to lift the gloom. After some persuasion, Dana eventually agreed. Martha even loaned her sister an outfit, a beige dress, a leopard print scarf, and a pair of black ankle boots.

Dana Fader was an attractive woman. She turned quite a few heads that night. And the night on the town proved to be just the ticket for lifting the alimony blues. The sisters visited several bars before Dana eventually called it a night. Martha then dropped her at the Willow Lakes Apartments complex. It was around 2 a.m. when Martha drove away, heading out for one last drink. Dana, meanwhile, headed upstairs. A short while later, Joseph Bailey was awakened by clattering from the kitchen and got up to find his slightly tipsy sister preparing a meal of sausage and eggs. Dana told him that she might pay a visit to her boyfriend, who lived in the same building. Joseph then went back to bed. When he woke again, just before 9 a.m., the smell of burned food pervaded the apartment.

The source of the stench was soon identified. Dana's pan was still on the stove, the sausages burned to a crisp. Somewhat mystified, Joseph conducted a quick search of the residence. His sister wasn't there. Dana's purse was on the kitchen table but of her, there was no trace. Somewhat anxious now, Joseph called at the apartment occupied by Dana's boyfriend. Dana wasn't there either. Joseph's next stop was at his mother's apartment. It was she who insisted that they call the police.

The mystery of Dana Fader's sudden disappearance would be resolved shortly after deputies arrived at the scene. Dana's 1980 Ford Fairmont was found parked on one side of the complex, with the keys in the ignition. Dana was inside, still wearing the beige dress that had drawn so many admiring glances the night before. Only now, the dress was hitched up over her waist and stained with blood and seminal fluid. Dana was in the back seat of her car, her legs spread and her eyes staring sightlessly ahead. There were ugly bruises on her slender throat. Dana Fader had been raped and murdered.

But how had this happened? How had the young woman gone from cooking herself a late-night meal to ending up dead in the parking lot? Detectives surmised that Dana must have come downstairs to fetch something from the car and been ambushed. The killer had then driven the vehicle to a quiet corner of the lot. There, he'd hung a blanket from the back passenger window to shield the scene from view. He'd then attacked Dana, raped her, and strangled her to death. The autopsy would find scratches and finger imprints on her neck. It would also detect a bite mark on one of the victim's nipples. This was a savage, animalistic murder.

Perpetrated by whom? That was the question. Was this a random attack, a tragic case of wrong place, wrong time, or had Dana known her killer? Since the latter is almost always the case in a murder inquiry, the police started there, questioning Dana's boyfriend, an ex with a history of domestic violence, even her brother. All of these suspects were cleared. When the most promising lead, a palm print found on the rear passenger window, also came up empty, the investigation was in trouble.

The police, of course, had a case-busting piece of evidence in their possession - the blood and seminal fluid retrieved from the crime scene. But this was of limited use back in the 1980s. DNA was only just emerging as a technology. It was prohibitively expensive and only effective under near-perfect conditions. The samples collected by Palm Beach County investigators were not yet viable. It would take 19 years of sustained scientific progress before a profile could be extracted. That was in 2006. Unfortunately, there was no match to be found at that time.

The Combined DNA Index System (CODIS) is a national database of DNA profiles created and maintained by the FBI. Actually, CODIS is a collection of databases, including missing persons, convicted offenders, and forensic samples from crime scenes. It is ever-expanding, so failure to find a hit the first time does not preclude a successful outcome at a later date. Law agencies know this and so requests may be submitted multiple times over the course of an investigation. In the Fader case, six years would pass before a second attempt was made. This time around, there was a match. The man who'd raped and murdered Dana Fader was a convicted rapist from Jackson, Mississippi. His name was Rodney Clark.

The crime that resulted in Rodney Clark's incarceration had occurred in Mississippi in 1988, just months after the murder of Dana Fader. The 18-year-old victim was snatched from a street, then subjected to a vicious sexual assault. Unlike Dana, she survived her ordeal to point out Clark as her attacker. Clark entered a guilty plea at trial and earned himself an eight-year stint in the penitentiary. This was how his DNA profile ended up in CODIS.

Brought in for questioning, Clark insisted that he'd never lived in Florida, outside of a brief stint in the Job Corps when he was 17. When that was proven to be a lie, he conceded that he had lived in Palm Beach in the mid-80s, and was still living there in 87, when

Dana Fader was murdered. However, he denied killing her. Shown a picture of the dead woman, his reaction was decidedly creepy. "She's pretty," he said, leering at the photograph, "But I've never seen her before in my life."

Despite these denials, Clark could not explain how his blood and semen had ended up on the body of a murder victim. He also could not explain how the palm print (now confirmed to be his) was on the rear window of the car in which the body had been found. All he could do was insist on his innocence. He was charged with first-degree murder anyway and extradited to Florida in 2013.

As the matter headed to trial, Clark continued to insist that the police had the wrong man. "They can have DNA," he told a reporter. "I ain't killed nobody. I don't give a damn what they got. I am innocent of any crime committed against Dana Fader." He also insisted that he looked forward to the trial, as an opportunity to "clear his name." His public defender took a rather more pragmatic view. Carey Haughwout knew how damaging the DNA evidence was to his case and fought hard to have it suppressed. Had he succeeded, Rodney Clark would undoubtedly have walked. Once the motion was denied, the writing was on the wall for Clark.

Rodney Clark appeared for trial in 2017, with the prosecutor determined to send him to death row. For Clark's defense team, there was only one option. They attacked the DNA evidence. This is seldom a winning strategy, and it wasn't in this case. Clark was convicted of first-degree murder. Then came the sentencing phase, with the defense producing a heavy hitter to argue for Clark's life. Dr. Jethro Toomer had appeared as an expert witness in the trials of Florida's two most notorious killers, Ted Bundy and Aileen Wuornos. Now he was here to argue that Rodney Clark did not deserve to die. Clark, he said, had suffered horrendous abuse as a child. That should be taken in mitigation.

And the jury agreed, perhaps swayed by the fact that Clark was now disabled and was wheeled into the courtroom each day in a wheelchair. Rather than the needle, Rodney Clark was sentenced to life in prison with no possibility of parole. For Dana Fader's family, the ruling came as a relief. Thirty years had passed since Dana's sister had taken her out for a night on the town, a night that had ended in tragedy. The road to justice had been long and torturous. It was over now.

Living the Low Life

James Wilfred Trotter was 13 years old, a handsome, blond kid known as Jamey to his friends and family. Jamey was outgoing and friendly. His older brother, Jeff, said that he could strike up a conversation with anyone. On April 19, 1979, that gregarious nature would get him into trouble. That was the day that Jamey got off a school bus near his home in Costa Mesa, California and disappeared. He was reported missing within hours, but the police were slow to respond and lax when they did eventually take action. They believed that Jamey had run away. Nothing that his mom, Barbara, could say would convince them otherwise.

Eleven years after Jamey Trotter disappeared, a hiker was walking a trail west of Lake Elsinore, when he came across a pile of charred bones. Riverside County deputies responded to the scene and verified that the bones were indeed human. Later, the medical examiner would form the opinion that they were from a young female and that they had been out in the open for at least a decade. That gave investigators a timeframe to work with, but they found no missing persons cases within that time frame that matched the criteria, no unsolved homicide to link to the remains. The bones ended up packed into an evidence locker where they would stay for the next six years.

Then, in 1996, detectives decided to take another look at the case and the bones were re-examined. This time, the pathologist formed a different opinion. He decided that the remains were not female after all, but that they belonged to a pre-pubescent male. There was also something the original examination had missed. The teeth still lodged in the jawbone showed evidence of dental work. It was by this method that investigators were eventually able to identify their John Doe. Seventeen years after he'd gone missing, Jamey Trotter had been found at last. This was now a murder inquiry.

But this would not be an easy case to solve. A long time had lapsed. Physical evidence that might have been left at the dumpsite had long since dissipated. There was no indication of where Jamey had been killed or even how he'd died. All that the police had to go on, was the hiker who had discovered the remains. They decided to start there. The man's name was James Crummel and, as the police were about to discover, he wasn't just some outdoor enthusiast who'd had the misfortune of stumbling on human remains in the wilderness. Crummel was a man with a dark and sordid past.

Born in Kalamazoo, Michigan in 1944, James Crummel was raised by a domineering mother who had wanted a daughter and who insisted on dressing him as a girl throughout his childhood. James had been close to his father, but Crummel Sr had died in a motorcycle accident when the boy was 14. Two years later, his mother remarried, and James developed a strained relationship with his stepfather. Sometimes, things devolved into physical violence. On one occasion, the police had to be called when James threatened to kill his stepfather with a meat cleaver. A short time after that incident, he left home for good, enlisting in the army at the age of 17.

It was while serving in the military that Crummel committed his first known offense. While stationed in Missouri in 1962, he lured two boys, aged 13 and 11, into the woods. There, he tied them to a tree and raped them. Crummel warned his victims not to say anything, but the boys reported the attack. At the subsequent trial, a psychologist testified that Crummel had the mental age of an 8-year-old. That assessment kept him out of jail, but his military career was over.

We next catch up with James Crummel in 1967, on the outskirts of Tucson, Arizona. Crummel lived in a mobile home here, with his partner Steve Shimer. Living close by, was an eight-year-old named Frank Clawson. In February of that year, Frank set off on his bicycle to visit a friend and never returned. A search was launched, and the boy was found the next morning, tossed into a ditch with his pants down and his belt pulled tightly around his neck. The autopsy would show that he had been strangled. He had also been sodomized. Just days later, with the police canvassing the area and questioning residents, Crummel and Shimer packed up their stuff and moved out of state. They ended up in Wisconsin, where Crummel was soon attracting the attention of the authorities.

In 1968, Crummel picked up a 14-year-old hitchhiker, drove him to a remote spot, and sexually assaulted him. He then started beating the boy with a tree branch, knocking him unconscious and causing horrific injuries. Eventually, he left, apparently believing his victim to be dead. But against all odds, the boy survived, crawled out of the ravine where he'd been dumped, and managed to flag down a passing motorist. Injured and traumatized, he was unable to talk for three days. When he did find his voice, he provided enough information to lead the police to James Crummel who was arrested and charged with sexual assault and attempted murder. For these grave charges, the sexual psychopath would serve less than five years in prison. He was free again in 1973, taking his lethal roadshow to Southern California.

And it is here that we find James Crummel on April 19, 1979, the day that 13-year-old Jamey Trotter went missing. As Riverside County detectives would find out in their 1996 cold case investigation, he'd lived just down the street from Jamey and his family. Yet, he was never connected to the murder and never would have been flagged as a person of interest but for his decision to inform the police of his 'discovery' of human remains.

Why would Crummel have done such a thing, putting himself in danger of being caught? It is because James Crummel was a psychopath, eager for the next thrill. Brutally ending the life of a 13-year-old wasn't enough for him. He also had to demonstrate his brilliance by leading the authorities to the gruesome evidence of his handiwork. He had to tempt them with the evidence and yet escape detection.

And Crummel had succeeded in that goal. For six years after the discovery of the skeletal remains, he had continued to fly under the radar. Now, though, the police had him in their sights. There was more to be uncovered in his murky past. Investigators were beginning to suspect that James Crummel might be a serial killer.

They'd have to move cautiously, though. Crummel was a slippery character who seemed to live a charmed life when it came to avoiding the consequences of his nefarious deeds. Back in 1982, Arizona prosecutors had believed that they finally had enough to nail him for the murder of Frank Clawson. Crummel was extradited from California and was due to stand trial. But then his former lover, Steve Shimer, recanted the statement he'd given, and the case collapsed. Crummel was free to go but he was soon in trouble again after he was caught molesting the nine-year-old son of a friend. He'd ultimately be found not guilty of that charge although he did serve 200 days for failing to register as a sex offender.

In February 1983, the state of Arizona had another crack at the Clawson case, this time securing a murder conviction. But the case was thrown out on appeal after a judge ruled that Crummel had not been adequately represented. Crummel ended up striking a deal with Pima County prosecutors, pleading down to kidnapping and accepting a three-year jail term. He walked free in 1987. In 1995, he was living in Big Bear City, California, when yet another young boy went missing.

Jack Phillips was only nine years old when he went for a walk to a park near his home and never returned. James Crummel, who was living just down the block at the time, somehow managed to avoid being flagged as a suspect. He would later boast to a cellmate that he had abducted, raped, and murdered the child.

But now, James Crummel's run of good fortune had finally come to an end. In June of 2004, he was convicted of the murder of James Trotter and sentenced to death. Crummel then tried to strike a deal with prosecutors, offering to give up the location of Jack Phillips' body in exchange for a commutation of sentence to life in prison. The state of California refused. Crummel was sent to San Quentin to await execution. Given California's paltry record of following through with executions, he would likely have remained there indefinitely. On May 27, 2012, James Crummel did the world a favor by hanging himself in his cell.

What we know for certain is that James Crummel was a serial killer, responsible for the deaths of at least three young boys. But that is not the full extent of Crummel's career of evil. He remains the prime suspect in the April 1979 disappearance of 7-year-old Charles Christopher Francis, from a street in Santa Ana, California. Crummel has also been connected to the disappearances of two teenagers from Cedu Therapeutic Boarding School in Running Springs, California, in the mid-90s. He was working there as a youth counselor when John Inman and Blake Wade Pursley went missing. Neither boy has ever been found.

After the Fire

Judith Delgros

In 1977, Donald Morris went to visit his parents in Florida and returned to his native Ohio with a wife. Donald was 41 years old, recently divorced, lonely, and desperate for female companionship. His new bride, Judith, was a two-time divorcee. She, too, had a motive, other than romance, for the whirlwind marriage. Her children had been removed from her care due to her inability to support them. With a husband in tow, she'd be able to get them back. Shortly after Judith moved into Donald's mobile home in Vernon Township, Ohio, she was joined by her sons, Christopher Styles, 5, John Styles, 6, and Edward Bridge, 9. Donald Morris hadn't just acquired a wife, he'd acquired an instant family.

But this was not a happy union. Judith was an argumentative woman and Donald wasn't one to back down from an altercation. The couple fought constantly and sometimes their disagreements turned violent. It did not take long for Donald to realize that he'd made a terrible mistake. He was starting to accept that a second excursion through the divorce courts might be necessary. Then, on the night of January 3, 1978, that decision was taken out of his hands. That was the night that his trailer caught fire.

The report of a residence ablaze on Orangeville-Kinsman Road came into the Burghill-Vernon fire department at 12:35 that morning. Firefighters were scrambled to the location but there was little they could do. The fire was already out of control. It would eventually require reinforcements from four local fire departments to put it out. Once they succeeded in that mammoth task, the remains of Donald Morris and 5-year-old Christopher Styles could be retrieved. Man and boy had died in separate rooms. The other three residents of the house, Judith Morris and her sons Edward and John had escaped. The boys had second-degree burns and were suffering the effects of smoke inhalation. Judith did not have a mark on her.

The trio was taken to a local hospital for treatment. There, detectives caught up with Judith and questioned her regarding the fire. According to Judith, she'd wakened to the smell of something burning and noticed smoke seeping under her bedroom door. She woke her husband and they exited into the hall. There they encountered a "wall of flame" blocking their way out through the living room. Turning right, they moved towards the rear of the house and exited through the back door. Donald then "threw her outside," and went back in, presumably to save the children. In the next moment, her son John came "flying into her arms."

Judith then ran next door to wake Donald's nephew, Gary. The smoke was now so thick that Gary had to crawl on all fours into the interior. Coughing and hacking, he dragged nine-year-old

Edward Bridge to safety. He then tried to go back in, but the fire was so intense that he was driven back. Donald Morris and Christopher Styles, still trapped inside, never stood a chance.

Not everyone in the Trumbull County Sheriff's Department was satisfied with this explanation. For starters, there was Judith's suggestion that the blaze had been caused by an exploding furnace. If that was the case, why hadn't everyone in the household been awakened? And why had none of the neighbors heard anything? Indeed, there was evidence that the fire had started in several different places throughout the home, rather than in a single location.

Then there was Judith's attire. According to her, she'd been asleep in bed when the fire started. Why then was she fully dressed when the first responders arrived? Judith's demeanor was also questioned. Paramedics reported that she'd been laughing in the ambulance on the way to the hospital. Was that really the behavior of a woman who'd just lost her husband and youngest son to a tragedy?

Each of these factors raised red flags with investigators. And there were other anomalies too, that might have raised questions. How was it that Judith alone had escaped the fire unscathed? And how come Donald Morris's ear had been severed? This was not an injury incurred in the blaze. The severed ear was found a short distance from the trailer, and it was not burnt at all. How had it been removed and how had it gotten there?

Still, even with these unanswered questions, there were only two opinions that counted. The coroner ruled the deaths accidental, and the fire chief concluded that the blaze was the result of a furnace explosion. The investigation was closed. Judith Morris could lay her husband and son to rest. By the end of that year, she had moved on with her life and remarried.

Dan D'Annunzio had been a sheriff's deputy at the time of the fatal fire and had worked on the case as an investigator. He'd been one of those who'd most loudly voiced his opinion that there was more to the case than Judith Morris was telling. Perhaps that was behind his reassignment to traffic duty shortly after the tragedy, perhaps not. In any event, D'Annunzio never forgot about the case. In 1993, having attained the rank of lieutenant, he decided to re-open it.

D'Annunzio's first step was to track down the survivors of the fire. His initial efforts focused on Edward Bridge, the oldest of Judith's sons. Finding Bridge was easy. He was currently incarcerated in Pennsylvania, where he was serving a jail term for rape. But Bridge was less than receptive to D'Annunzio's overtures. In fact, he was downright hostile. "Why do you want to bring this up now?" he demanded. "Why after all these years?" It would take all of D'Annunzio's powers of persuasion to get him to eventually open up.

But open up he did, and what he had to say was explosive. According to Bridge, his mother and stepfather had been arguing that day, with Donald accusing his wife of cheating on him. That night, as they continued sniping at each other, Judith put her sons to bed after forcing them to each swallow four teaspoons of cough syrup. This, according to a medical expert who testified at the trial, would have been enough to induce sleep in the youngsters. Certainly, it had knocked out Edward Bridge.

But Edward had woken a few hours later, needing to go to the bathroom. Leaving his room, he'd heard raised voices – his mother and stepfather still going at it. Peering into their bedroom as he passed, he'd seen Donald slap his mother. Then his mom picked something up and struck Donald on the head, knocking him to the floor. As he lay there, Judith left the room and ran down the passage to the kitchen. When she returned, she was holding a knife. Edward saw her re-enter the room, watched as she plunged the blade four or five times into Donald's back. A short while later, Bridge claimed, he saw his mother pouring something into the furnace.

The story was patchy in places and seemed somewhat contrived. Given that it was told by a convicted rapist who'd been just nine years old at the time and, by his own admission, doped with cough syrup, it was far from enough to bring murder charges. But it was enough to obtain an exhumation order on the bodies of Donald Morris and Christopher Styles.

Those bodies had now been 15 years in the ground and were badly decomposed. Still, the telltale signs were there for the pathologist to find. Four of Donald's ribs were sliced through and one of his vertebrae had been nicked. These were injuries consistent with a knife being plunged with considerable force into his back. There was also evidence that he had bled profusely before he died.

With the forensics in hand, plus Edward Bridge's testimony to
back it up, prosecutors sought and obtained a grand jury
indictment against Judith Morris. Now going by her married name
Delgros, and living in Sharon, Ohio, Judith was arrested at her
workplace on March 22, 1993. She was charged with the murders
of her former husband and five-year-old son.

The trial would pit brother against brother, as Edward Bridge
testified for the prosecution and John Styles spoke in his mother's
defense, insisting that she was "incapable of murder" and had
saved his life on that fateful night. The proceedings then took a
bizarre turn when the prosecutor suggested that Judith Delgros
was a practicing witch, and that witchcraft might have been a
motive for the murders. Donald Morris's severed ear was cited as
evidence of this, but it is doubtful that the jury took these
insinuations seriously.

The murders had a far more practical explanation. Judith had
decided to rid herself of a troublesome husband and of parental
responsibilities at the same time. But for her son's late-night
bathroom break and the brave efforts of Gary Morris, she might
well have succeeded.

In the end, it all came down to the evidence. Donald Morris had
undoubtedly been stabbed to death and there was only one person
who could have inflicted those injuries. That made Judith's story of
the fire a fabrication and why would she have told the lie other
than to cover up her role in starting the blaze?

Judith Delgros was ultimately convicted of two counts of murder and sentenced to life in prison. Parole was not ruled out and Delgros is now eligible. She was turned down at her first hearing in 2013. Now in her early seventies, she remains an inmate at the Ohio Reformatory for Women.

Evil Eyes

In the west central Lowlands of Scotland, on the banks of the River Clyde, sits the town of Greenock, a picturesque burgh of just over 40,000 souls. These days, it's a relatively tranquil place, relying on banking, insurance, and the call center industry to fund its civic coffers. But it wasn't always so. In earlier times, Greenock was a hub of heavy industry, most specifically, shipbuilding. Back in 1986, when our story takes place, the town was caught somewhere between these eras of prosperity. The shipyards were gone, the service industries yet to arrive. Unemployment was the norm and its evil twin, crime, was rampant. Mostly, these were property-related offenses but there was violence too, mainly confined to the rough-and-tumble east end. The west side of town kept to a more genteel, middle-class standard. Within these leafy climes, on a thoroughfare called Ardgowan Street, lived a girl named Elaine Doyle.

Elaine was a responsible young woman. Just 16 years old, she had already embarked on her working career, clerking behind the counter at a local jewelry store. She lived at home with her parents who knew her to be a good girl, a happy girl. Pretty and dark-haired, Elaine was also popular with her peer group. On the night of Sunday, June 1,

1986, she decided to accompany a friend to a disco, hosted by the local chapter of the Celtic Supporters Club. Elaine was actually too young to attend, but her parents had no qualms about allowing her to go. The club was a walkable distance from home and Elaine was a mature young woman who'd never given them cause for concern. She said her goodbyes that night, promising to be home by no later than 1 a.m. The last words that her father spoke to her were, "Take care."

The following morning, Jack and Maureen Doyle woke to find that their daughter had not returned during the night. They were not unduly concerned by this. Elaine sometimes slept over at a friend's place when she did not want to disturb them by coming in late. On this particular morning, there was also a distraction, just down the street there was a hive of activity, dozens of police officers hovering around the entrance to a narrow lane, about 40 yards from their front door. Jack and Maureen did not make the connection between the police activity and their missing daughter until an officer knocked on their door. A young girl's body had been found in the lane, naked, her clothing neatly folded and placed on the ground beside her. Then the officer described the clothes and the Doyles' world collapsed in around them – a black and white dress, a blue leather jacket, the exact outfit that Elaine had worn for her night out.

Elaine's body had been found at around 7 a.m. that morning, by a local man who'd been walking to his car. He'd immediately gone back inside and called the police, who soon arrived to cordon off the area. Officers then started canvassing the neighborhood, while forensic experts began processing the scene. Given the state of the body, this was clearly a sexually motivated crime although, curiously, there was no semen. The forensic team also attempted to retrieve hairs and fibers from the victim, using the primitive, yet effective, method favored in those days. This involved running strips of sticky tape over the skin in the hope of picking up microscopic trace evidence. In this case, they found nothing that could be processed with the technology of the day. The strips were nonetheless bagged and placed in storage.

Later that day, Elaine's body would be removed to the morgue where it was determined that she'd been killed by ligature strangulation. Someone had looped a length of rope around her neck and pulled it tight enough to deprive her of oxygen. Who, though? Who could have done such a terrible thing to an innocent, young girl?

That was the question that the Strathclyde Police had to answer, and they appeared to get an early break when several witnesses reported that they'd seen a red-haired man sprinting through the darkened streets. This man was elevated to the top of the suspect list, with the local newspaper, the Greenock Telegraph, running an identikit picture on its front page. Another eyewitness report, of a young, dark-haired man with large "staring" eyes, was all but ignored. Meanwhile, a massive operation was underway, with police working the route that Elaine would have taken. Additional officers were brought in from across the west of Scotland. Between them, they'd knock on over 2,300 doors and take nearly 4,500 statements. It was all to no avail. Time for the local police to admit defeat and call in the Serious Crimes Squad.

The murder of Elaine Doyle sparked panic in Greenock. This was a town with a high crime rate but a negligible rate of murder. Certainly, the seemingly random killing of a west-side teenager was a rarity. For a time, there were genuine fears that a psycho killer was living among them and might strike again. But as weeks turned into months, those fears began to wane. The failure of the police to arrest a local suspect now led many to believe that the fiend wasn't one of their own, after all. The consensus seemed to be that he was probably a trucker, passing through the area when Elaine Doyle had the misfortune of encountering him.

This convenient theory would soon be accepted as fact. Then, a few weeks after the murder, it would be debunked in a stark demonstration. A leather handbag was found smoldering on the steps of the town library, the same bag that Elaine had been carrying on the night she was killed. The killer had apparently held on to it since that date and was now returning it in theatrical fashion. To what purpose? Was this just an attention-seeking stunt? Was it a warning that he was still around and might strike again? No one knew and that only added to the panic that rippled through the town.

As it turned out, the handbag incident was the last that the people of Greenock would hear from their local boogeyman for over two decades. The Serious Crimes Unit had fared no better than the local cops in tracking him down and eventually the investigation was scaled back, then shut down completely. It would remain in this dormant state until 2012, when the police launched Operation Evergreen, aimed at bringing the Greenock strangler to justice.

This was not some tentative inquiry, carried out by a couple of detectives in a back room. This was a massive undertaking, involving 40 officers, with the full resources of Police Scotland at their disposal. Still, they faced an uphill battle. There were over 14,000 witness statements to go through, hoping for some small shred of evidence that the original investigative team might have missed. There was also, of course, the forensic evidence. It was this that would provide the first break. On one of the strips of sticky tape, the lab detected the DNA profile of an unknown male.

Had there been a match to this profile on the available databases, then the case could have been closed right there. But things seldom come easy in an investigation this old. No match was found. The Operation Evergreen team was going to have to do this the hard way. It would have to track down every man who'd been interviewed as a potential suspect at the time of the original inquiry. There were 722 of them and some had since died or left the area.

One of the men who'd been interviewed back then was an individual named John Doherty. A local man, Doherty had lived all his life in Greenock, save for a couple of years in the late 80s when he'd served in the British Army. Now 49 years old, Doherty was a married man and a father of one, working as a truck driver for the local council. He had an unblemished police record and was known to neighbors and co-workers as a quiet and unassuming individual. In short, he was the last person anyone would suspect of murder.

But Doherty was on the list and so a couple of detectives arrived at his home to question him. Back in 1986, when the police issued an appeal for anyone who'd been at the Celtic club to come forward, Doherty had not complied. It was a friend who'd placed him at the Sunday night disco. Now, Doherty told the officers that he had been present. He even admitted that he was a former classmate of Elaine's brother, also named John. However, he claimed that he had not known Elaine. He was then asked to provide a DNA swab and agreed to do so. It was this swab that would crack the decades-old case. It was a match to the DNA lifted from Elaine's body. Later, when a photo array was presented to the eyewitness who'd seen the man with the "staring" eyes, he picked out Doherty without a moment's hesitation. Even after all these years, he said, he could not get those "evil eyes" out of his mind.

Arrested and charged with murder, John Doherty appeared at the Edinburgh High Court in 2014. There, his barrister challenged the validity of the DNA evidence, claiming that it was degraded and had been mishandled by police officers. That was perhaps the only option open to the defense, but it turned out to be a losing strategy. John Doherty showed little emotion as he was convicted and sentenced to life in prison, with a minimum of 21 years.

Justice had been a long time coming for the Doyle family. Sadly, it did not come soon enough for Elaine's dad, Jack. He had died years earlier, never knowing who had snuffed out the life of his beloved daughter. The motive for this terrible crime remains a mystery.

If You Tell

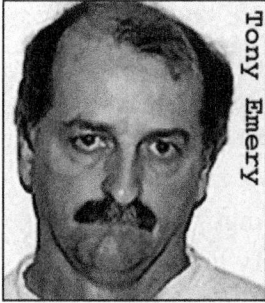

Maryville, Missouri is a typical small Midwestern town, a sleepy rural burg where hardly anything of note ever happens. But back in the early 90s, the jurisdiction was dealing with a serious methamphetamine problem. So serious that agents of the Bureau of Alcohol, Firearms, and Tobacco (ATF) got involved. The first thing that these investigators did, was to determine who the main narcotics supplier was in the area. That was easily established. Everyone knew that local drug lord, Tony Emery had cornered the market.

Next, the Feds sought out a weak link in Emery's supply chain and zoned in on Christine Elkins, a 32-year-old mother of two, whose meth habit had forced her into some desperate measures. Christine had taken to running drugs for Tony Emery to fund her own consumption. Picked up on possession with intent to distribute, she was given a stark choice, cooperate or face a long prison term. She chose to cooperate.

The first task that the ATF assigned to Christine was a tough one. They asked her to wear a wire to her next meeting with Emery.

Christine was less than keen on the idea. She knew what Tony was like. He was a ruthless man who would not take kindly to betrayal. If he even suspected that she was wired, she'd be in deep trouble.

But Christine had little choice in the matter and so she agreed to be fitted with the recording device. In the movies, this usually plays out with the criminal mastermind revealing all about his unlawful activities, providing investigators with everything they need to bring him down. But real life isn't like Hollywood. Emery immediately picked up on Christine's nervous demeanor and asked outright if she was wearing a wire. Christine said no and Emery then warned that he'd kill her if he ever found out that she'd betrayed him.

Christine Elkins left that meeting understandably shaken. In fact, she was so traumatized that her handlers pulled her from the case. They would still require her to testify against Emery once they got him in front of a judge and jury but, for now, she was off the hook. Only, the Feds had badly underestimated just how much the encounter with Emery had terrified Christine. There was no way she was ever going to take the stand against him in a court of law.

In early August 1990, Christine Elkins asked a friend to look after her sons while she went to a meeting. She wouldn't say who she was going to see but she was quite obviously anxious. "If I don't come back, you'll find me at the morgue," she told her friend. She did not know just how prophetic those words would turn out to be.

Christine drove away in her maroon, two-door Oldsmobile Cutlass that day and was never seen again. A search was launched for her, of course, one that involved local cops, the ATF, and the Missouri State Police. It came up empty. Christine had vanished from the face of the earth. More than likely, Tony Emery had gotten to her and if that was the case, she was probably lying in a shallow grave somewhere. That theory was given credence three weeks after Christine's disappearance when an inmate named James Witt provided a tip-off to investigators. Witt was a methamphetamine cook and a one-time associate of Tony Emery and his cousin Herb. According to him, he'd heard Tony and Herb discussing the murder of a female informant. In exchange for a sentencing consideration, he'd be prepared to meet with Herb and get him to admit to the murder on tape.

And so, a deal was struck. Three months after Christine Elkins went missing, James Witt met with Herb Emery in a restaurant parking lot, while ATF agents sat in a van nearby, listening in. Witt was more practiced at this kind of deception than Christine. He did not ask Herb directly about the murder. To do so would arouse suspicion. Instead, he told Herb that he had a body to dispose of and asked for the best method of doing so. Herb said that he should place the corpse into the trunk of a car and then sink it to the bottom of a rock quarry. He hinted that it was a method he'd used in the past.

It wasn't an admission of murder, but it did at least give a hint as to what might have happened to Christine. Based on what Herb Emery had said, it seemed likely that she and her vehicle had been submerged in a body of water in the area. The next step was to identify potential sites. There are hundreds of water-logged quarries scattered across the Midwest, but the investigators reckoned that the Emerys would not have driven too far from their home base. To do so would put them at risk of being pulled over in a random traffic stop. Then they'd be caught red-handed with a corpse in the trunk.

The search area was thus restricted to a 75-mile radius around Maryville. That still left dozens of locations to search but the cops went about it methodically, ticking off one location after the other. The operation would take several months to complete. By the end of it, they were left empty-handed.

The search for Christine Elkins had failed but the operation to nail Tony Emery on drugs charges went on. Fortunately, the police now had an insider in Emery's operation. James Witt was still playing ball. In the summer of 1991, a sting was set up. Witt arranged to sell several pounds of meth to Emery for $20,000. The transaction was completed under the surveillance of ATF agents and caught on camera. Tony and Herb Emery were arrested on the spot. They were later convicted of conspiracy to sell methamphetamine and sentenced to nine years in federal prison.

But still, the cops were dissatisfied. Tony Emery wasn't just a drug dealer, he was a killer. He needed to answer for the murder of Christine Elkins. With the cousins now safely behind bars, focus shifted to solving that homicide. A name had come up during James Witt's taped conversations with Herb. Bobby Miller was a known associate of the Emerys who was currently serving a jail term in Colorado. Investigators believed that he might have been present when Christine was killed and tried to get him to talk about it. Miller was offered a deal but was so terrified of Tony that he refused to say anything.

Six years passed without progress in the case. Then, in September 1996, came an unexpected break. Bobby Miller's lawyer contacted the

ATF and said that Miller was willing to speak in exchange for full immunity on murder charges. A deal was struck, and Miller provided investigators with the first clue as to Christine Elkins' fate.

According to Miller, Tony Emery had told him to hire a truck that day and bring it to his property in Maryville. Miller was sitting in the vehicle when Christine arrived, driving her maroon Cutlass. He saw her enter the building. Moments later, he heard screams coming from the house. Panicked, he started up the truck and drove away. That, Miller insisted, was all he knew.

The lack of detail in this account was frustrating to investigators. But at least they could now place Christine in the company of Tony and Herb Emery on the night she disappeared. It wasn't much but it was a start. Next, they began looking into other associates of the Emery cousins. That is what led them to Dana Kleiser.

Kleiser wasn't involved at all in the Emerys' criminal enterprise. His only connection to the cousins was that Tony had once dated his sister. However, he did have important information about the night Christine went missing. According to Kleiser, Tony had arrived at his home that night, wanting to borrow some gas. He'd then asked for the location of the nearest boat ramp. Wary of Emery's reputation, Kleiser wasn't about to question him on the issue. He agreed to accompany him to a ramp on the Missouri River. Once he'd done so, Emery told him to leave.

It was all starting to fall into place now. Investigators believed that Christine had agreed to meet with Tony Emery that night, probably to reassure him of her loyalty. However, she'd walked straight into a trap. Tony and Herb were waiting for her and killed her inside Tony's rented property. They then loaded her body into the trunk of her Cutlass and drove to the Missouri River, Herb at the wheel of Christine's car, Tony following. Tony had stopped at Dana Kleiser's home, asking for directions to the boat ramp. Then, after Kleiser left, they consigned the Cutlass to the murky depths of the Missouri, with Christine inside. All the investigators had to do now was recover the vehicle and they'd be able to make their case.

But herein lay the problem. Christine had disappeared in 1990, almost seven years ago. In 1993, Missouri had suffered some of its worst flooding in modern history. The river had burst its banks, leaving approximately 320,000 square miles underwater and causing an estimated $15 billion in damages. The Missouri is a fast-flowing river under normal circumstances, but the flood had turned it into a raging torrent, more than capable of sweeping a submerged car away. For all the police knew, the vehicle might be in the Gulf of Mexico by now.

And so, the ATF turned to outside experts, enlisting the help of a non-profit organization called NecroSearch. This Colorado-based group of scientists helps law enforcement agencies to locate clandestine graves and hidden bodies. In this case, they started by surveying the river, using currents and depths to calculate the best place to look. It came down to a six-mile stretch of water, downstream of the boat ramp. Here, they employed an instrument called a magnetometer, a torpedo-shaped device that measures changes in magnetic fields under the water. Incredibly, eleven cars were located along this short stretch of river. Divers were then sent to the depths to get a visual on the vehicles. Within hours, one of them surfaced, holding a Missouri license plate aloft. Christine Elkins' car had been found.

Brought to the surface, the vehicle would give up its macabre secret. Christine's body was in the trunk, wrapped in a carpet. She had not died easy. The autopsy would identify severe fractures and a large hole in her skull. Christine had been beaten to death with some blunt instrument.

Tony and Herb Emery were just weeks away from freedom when investigators arrived with murder warrants. Faced with the prospect of life without parole, Herb cracked, struck a deal with prosecutors, and agreed to testify against his cousin. According to Herb, Tony had lured Christine to his house that night by offering to pay her off in exchange for her silence. However, it was never his intention to make good on that promise. The plan was always to secure her silence the old-fashioned way, by assuring that she'd never be able to tell. Herb swore that he had not laid a hand on Christine. Tony had insisted on taking care of her himself. He'd beaten her to death with a heavy-duty flashlight.

Herb Emery entered a guilty plea at his trial and accepted a term of 22 years behind bars. Tony Emery was convicted of first-degree murder and sentenced to life without parole. His days as a ruthless thug, a drug dealer, a cold-hearted killer, are done. He will die behind bars.

Poetry in Justice

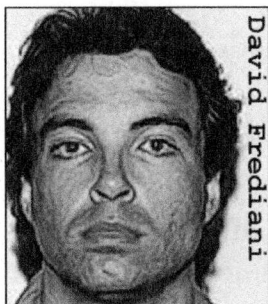

David Frediani

Dr. Helena Greenwood was a brilliant woman. A native of England, daughter of a geologist and a university professor, Helena had exhibited a keen intellect from an early age. As a teen, she'd developed an interest in chemistry and had gone on to obtain a doctorate in chemical pathology at the age of just 26. Aside from that, she was an incredibly determined woman, recognized by her peers and teachers as someone who was going to make her mark on the world. In the early 80s, she brought her talents to the United States, where there was a biotech boom underway. She and her husband Roger settled in Palo Alto, where Helena was quickly snapped up by the Syva Company, an energetic startup that was taking on the industry giants in the profitable medical diagnostics business.

To say that Helena was a success at her new job would be an understatement. In no time at all, she'd risen to the position of international marketing director. This was a high-pressure job. Helena was constantly on the go, consulting with scientists and physicians all over the world. Her outgoing nature and networking skills made her a natural. Back at the office, meanwhile, she developed a reputation as a hard taskmaster, someone who demanded high standards of herself and of those who reported to her. Her employers would later attribute the survival of the company during these turbulent times almost entirely to Helena's efforts.

It wasn't all work and no play, though. Helena and Roger had an intense personal relationship. They enjoyed sailing and often took a boat out along the coast. They were also fixing up the starter home they'd bought in Atherton, an upscale suburb near San Francisco. Here, Roger, a landscape architect, was planting a typical English garden. The couple was happy and thriving. Then, on the night of Saturday, April 7, 1984, the sanctity of their life and marriage would be violently snatched away.

Roger was out of town that day, having flown to Washington, D.C. on business. Home alone, Helena caught up on some paperwork before retiring at around 10:20 p.m. As was her habit, she read for a while before turning out the lights. She was rudely awakened about an hour later to find a man standing in the shadows of her bedroom. The man was tall, wearing a hoodie pulled tightly around his face. All that was visible, was his eyes. He held a flashlight in his right hand, a gun in his left. Guessing his intentions, Helena pulled the bedclothes tightly around her, hoping that would protect her. It did not. The man brandished the gun and warned her to cooperate if she wanted to live. In the end, Helena had no choice but to submit.

Afterward, after she'd been humiliated and violated, after her attacker had fled, Helena called a friend, Tom Christopher, who called the police and drove her to the hospital. She would spend the night with Tom's family in Oakland. The next day, Tom drove her back to the house in Atherton to collect some clothes. It was while they were there that Tom noticed a decorative teapot sitting on the deck. He pointed this out to Helena who noted that the pot was usually placed on the windowsill. The intruder had obviously moved it while gaining entry to the house. That meant that the teapot might have fingerprints on it. Tom immediately called the police, and a print was, indeed, lifted. It was the only one that would be found at the scene.

Unfortunately, the print did not find a match in police records. It would remain on file for ten months until a seemingly unrelated crime caught the attention of investigators. The perpetrator was an adult man who had been caught masturbating outside the bedroom window of a 13-year-old girl. What was noteworthy was the man's attire, a hoodie pulled tightly around his face, leaving only his eyes exposed. This was exactly how Helena Greenwood had described her assailant. On a whim, a detective compared the perp's fingerprints to the one lifted from the Greenwood crime scene. It was a match. Helena Greenwood's rapist had been caught. His name was David Paul Frediani.

Frediani was an anomaly to law enforcement. This wasn't your standard home-invading pervert. This was a presentable 30-year-old man with no priors, a college-educated accountant who worked for Pacific Telephone in San Francisco as a financial analyst. Still, the evidence was indisputable. Frediani's fingerprints had been found at the Greenwood residence. It was he who had attacked Helena Greenwood.

Brought into an interrogation room, Frediani appeared arrogant as investigators questioned him about the indecent exposure incident. His demeanor changed markedly when they switched gears and started asking about the attack on Helena Greenwood. Frediani seemed shocked at first. Then he regained his composure and said he had nothing to do with it. That denial lasted only until he was informed that his fingerprints had been found at the scene. Then he was flailing again. "I was drunk," he blurted. "I didn't know what I was doing." Finally, he clammed up and refused to say any more without his attorney present.

Frediani was charged with forcible oral copulation, burglary, and the use of a gun to commit a sex offense. He entered a guilty plea and was released on bail. In May 1985, Helena Greenwood testified at his preliminary hearing. Although she hadn't seen his face and couldn't positively identify him as her attacker, that wasn't really needed. The prosecution had his fingerprint at the scene and his sperm on Helena's pillowcase. Blood type analysis narrowed the serology down to one in seven men. In those pre-DNA days, that was about as good as it got. The trial was scheduled for September 1985. By that time, Helena Greenwood had moved south to San Diego, accepting a position at Gen-Probe, a company that specialized in DNA gene sequencing.

Thursday, August 22, 1985, was a beautiful day in Del Mar, the San Diego suburb where Helena and Roger had settled into a new house. Roger left for his office as usual that morning, driving away just before 8 p.m. Helena was due to follow soon after. She had an early meeting at Gen-Probe. On this day, however, the ultra-reliable, ultra-dependable Helena failed to show.

As the morning wore on with no sign of Helena, her colleagues grew increasingly concerned. Finally, a call was made to Roger, who left work and drove home to check on her. When he arrived, Roger found that he couldn't open the gate to the front yard. Something was wedged up against it and Roger soon discovered what that something was. It was his wife's body.

Helena Greenwood had been strangled, throttled to death in her own yard. The crime seemed entirely motiveless. Helena hadn't been robbed and she hadn't been sexually assaulted. Of course, there was one person who had a powerful reason for wanting her dead. That person was David Frediani. Helena had been due to testify at his sexual assault trial in just a matter of weeks.

As detectives started looking into Frediani's movements around the time of the murder, alarm bells began to jangle ever louder. On August 17, one week before Helena was killed, he'd been involved in a fender-bender in Los Angeles. What had he been doing this far south of his usual stomping ground in the Bay Area? Questioned about this, Frediani provided a smug and indolent answer. He said that he'd been driving towards Lake Tahoe when he'd decided, on a whim, to head for L.A. instead. It was almost as though he were taunting the cops, challenging them to prove that he was lying. The problem was, they couldn't.

David Frediani's sexual assault trial went ahead as scheduled in the fall of 1985. And if Frediani thought that Helena's death would derail the prosecution in any way, he was to be proven wrong. The testimony Helena had given at the preliminary hearing was admitted into evidence and Frediani was found guilty. That verdict was subsequently set aside on a technicality, but Frediani must have known that a new jury was likely to come to the same conclusion. Rather than go through the process again, he struck a deal and accepted a six-year jail term. He was out in three.

As for the murder investigation, that had ground to a shuddering halt. Investigators were certain that David Frediani was their killer but frustratingly aware that they lacked the evidence to prove it. Eventually, the case went cold. The files were sent to the homicide archives at the San Diego County Sheriff's Department, where they were stashed away with hundreds of other unsolved cases. They would remain there for 14 years, until the department's cold case squad decided to have another crack at bringing a killer to justice.

The Greenwood case was an excellent candidate for cold case review. Helena Greenwood had not gone meekly to her death. She'd lashed out at her attacker, removing a thin layer of skin cells. Those cells had been retrieved from under her fingernails during the original investigation. The minuscule sample had remained in an evidence vial all these years, waiting for technology to catch up. By 1999, it had. The newly discovered PCR method made it possible to retrieve DNA from tiny samples, even samples that were decades old. Nobody was really surprised when the profile was matched to David Frediani.

David Paul Frediani was convicted of the murder of Dr. Helena Greenwood in December 1999. He was sentenced to life in prison with no possibility of parole. There is a bittersweet irony in the fact that he was caught by DNA, the very technology that his victim was working on at the time of her death. It also brings a certain comfort to consider that Helena might have purposely scratched him, knowing that the skin cells would eventually nail him for her murder. Sometimes, there is poetry in justice.

40,000 Suspects

Roosevelt Gipson

It is one of the most popular shows on TV, a unique spin on the police procedural that focuses on the work of NCIS, the Naval Criminal Investigative Service. After a slow start, it has racked up 18 seasons (so far) and spawned three spin-offs. One of those is based in New Orleans and features a lead character named Dwayne Pride. What you may not know, is that Pride is inspired by a real person. His name is D'Wayne Swear and he served 22 years as a Special Agent with NCIS. These days, Swear is retired from law enforcement and acts as a consultant on the show. His job is to ensure realism and judging by the reviews, he does that well. Back in the 90s, however, Special Agent Swear was knee-deep in a homicide. It would become one of the headline cases of his career.

It started with the discovery of a corpse, floating face down in Lake O'Neill on the US Marine Corps base at Camp Pendleton, California. The victim was a slim, African American woman judged to be in her late 20s to early 30s. She was dressed in only a bra and panties, which had been pulled down to her knees. Cause of death was determined to be strangulation and blunt force trauma to the head. But who was she? Fingerprints would answer that question. The dead woman was

Marilyn Allen, a 30-year-old mother-of-four from Ohio who had
abandoned her family and moved out west. Her current residence was
in Oceanside, where she'd been picked up several times for
prostitution.

From the start, it was clear that this was going to be a difficult case to
solve. There was no DNA, no tire tracks, no foot impressions left in
the soft sand of the lakeshore. That suggested that the victim had been
killed off base and then driven to the lake and discarded there. Since
access to a military base is strictly controlled, it reduced the suspect
pool but not by much. Over 40,000 Marines are stationed at Camp
Pendleton, plus a small army of civilian workers. NCIS was up against
it from the start. Agents worked the case hard, running down the scant
leads they had. They never got close to identifying a suspect.

Over the years that followed, the civilian authorities would also take a
crack at the case, with a similar lack of success. Jurisdiction would
pass back and forth several times, further complicating matters. In the
end, the case went cold. At this stage, there seemed little possibility
that it would ever be solved.

Then, in 1999, there was an unexpected break. A young woman named
Seanice Etienne contacted the police in Baton Rouge, Louisiana, with
an interesting story to tell. According to Seanice, she'd recently started
dating a man named Roosevelt Gipson, a former Marine who'd quit
the Corps and now earned his living as a maintenance man on a
riverboat. Gipson was extremely charming and had swept the 20-year-
old college student off her feet during the early days of their
relationship, showering her with gifts. But a few weeks in and a dark
side had begun to emerge. He'd started hinting that he'd done some

'dark things' while he was in the Corps. Things that he was not proud of.

Seanice had automatically assumed that the things he was talking about had to do with military operations. She'd tried to reassure him, telling him that everyone has things in their lives they'd rather not have done. "Don't beat yourself up over it," was the advice she'd given. "No, you don't understand," Gipson had responded. "This is really bad."

A few weeks later, Seanice Etienne would discover just how bad. That was when Gipson confessed to her that he'd killed a woman in California and thrown her body into a lake. According to him, he'd grabbed the woman by the throat during an argument and had started strangling her. The woman had fought back but Gipson had slammed her head several times into the dashboard, knocking her unconscious. He'd then finished the job with his hands on her throat. Then, after fretting over what to do with the body, he'd loaded her into the trunk, driven onto the Camp Pendleton military base, and thrown her into a lake.

Seanice Etienne did not believe her new boyfriend's story at first. He just didn't seem the type. And why would he confess such a terrible crime to someone he'd known for only a few weeks? No, Seanice decided, he was making this up, even if she couldn't quite understand his motive for doing so.

But then came the incident that would convince her that Gipson might be telling the truth after all. It happened during their first argument as a couple. They were sitting in Gipson's car at the time and, as things became heated, he shot out a hand and grabbed her by the throat. "You see this finger right here?" he told her, wiggling one of his digits without loosening his grip, "I move this finger in a certain way and you'll be dead in 30 seconds, just like the other one."

Thankfully, Gipson did not follow through on his threat that night. But what about the next time he lost his temper? It was this terrifying prospect that convinced Seanice to call the police. They, in turn, contacted NCIS in San Diego. It did not take long to match the details Gipson had shared to the unsolved Marilyn Allen case. The case was then referred to the NCIS station in Baton Rouge, where Roosevelt Gipson was currently living. That was when Agent D'Wayne Swear got involved.

On the face of it, this was a straightforward matter. A man had confessed to murder, providing details that exactly matched an unsolved homicide. Case closed, right? Well, not quite. Gipson's 'confession' to Seanice Etienne would never stand up in a court of law, not without corroborating evidence, of which there was none. The only way to make the case would be for Gipson to confess his guilt on tape. That was going to require an undercover operation and Swear knew just the man for the job.

The United States Marine Corps is one of the world's elite fighting forces, a unit with a long and storied history. Marines have a unique bond, one with the other. This is a brotherhood forged in battle, affirmed in blood. If Gipson was going to open up to anyone, it would be to a fellow Marine.

And so, Swear turned to Jeff Winn a lieutenant with the New Orleans Police Department, who happened to be a close friend of his. Winn was also a gunnery sergeant with the Marine Corps Reserves and the first person that Swear thought of when it came to running his sting operation. Only, Winn wasn't interested. He'd worked undercover before and knew the toll it took on an officer, let alone on his family. He responded with an emphatic 'no,' when Swear first pitched the idea to him. It would take all of Swear's powers of persuasion to talk him around.

For the purposes of the operation, Lieutenant Winn would become a maintenance man at the riverboat casino. There, he soon befriended his work colleague and fellow Marine, Roosevelt Gipson. In his covert persona, Winn was an embittered divorcee engaged in a battle with his ex over child custody and alimony. He was also a man with anger management issues. His way of blowing off steam was to reminisce about his days in the Marines, the firefights he'd been involved in and the fringe actions, outside the Corps, some of them criminal. He found a willing audience, and contributor, in Gipson. He had his own demons to deal with, his own tales to tell. Only, he wasn't sharing the one story that investigators wanted on tape, the story of how he'd murdered Marilyn Allen.

The key component in an operation of this kind is patience. The suspect needs to be given room, to open up on his own terms. To push or to coax is to throw away all the hard work you've put in. Winn knew this and held back. He sensed that he was winning Gipson's trust. He was right in that assumption. One day, during a lunch break at work, Gipson started talking.

"Something happened to me at Camp Pendleton," he told his new friend. "It wasn't planned. It just kind of happened." Gipson went on to describe how he'd picked up a prostitute in Oceanside back in 1992. He paid her $10 to perform oral sex on him but wasn't happy with her performance and so the two of them got into an argument inside his vehicle. "I grabbed her by the throat," he told Winn. "And I just squeezed and squeezed."

But the woman wasn't giving up without a fight. She slid down in the passenger seat and kicked out, cracking the windshield. Gipson then slammed her head repeatedly into the dash, knocking her out. "I didn't think about it," he said. "She pissed me off." His voice resonated with anger as he made this statement. It was as though he were reliving the terrible events of that September night. He finished his story by telling how he'd snuck the body into the base in the trunk of his car and put her in the water. Every word was caught on tape. In February of 2000, Roosevelt Gipson was arrested and charged with the murder of Marilyn Allen.

Gipson was sent back to San Diego to face trial for murder. First, though, he'd have to undergo a psychiatric evaluation, to see if he was mentally competent to appear before a judge and jury. The defense was carrying an ace up its sleeve. Gipson had a history of mental illness and was a diagnosed paranoid schizophrenic. In the end, though, the decision went against him. He was ruled competent to stand trial. He was going to have to answer for snuffing out Marilyn Allen's life.

Jury trials can be tricky things. In this one, Assistant District Attorney Mike Still had a tough case to prove. Despite Gipson's admission of guilt, caught on tape and played in the courtroom, there was no corroborating evidence, no forensics, no witnesses. Perhaps that was behind the jury's decision to acquit Gipson of murder and convict him of manslaughter instead.

Roosevelt Gipson was sentenced to 11 years in prison and served only five years before he walked free. Thereafter, he moved to Las Vegas, Nevada. He died there on August 20, 2017, at the age of 45. His death was attributed to complications arising from AIDS.

Murder and Mayhem

Horst Eppenbach was the kind of guy you'd be proud to call a friend, the kind of guy you'd enjoy sitting down to a beer with, the kind of guy you could turn to in a crisis. A native of Baden-Württemberg, Germany, Horst had immigrated to America in the 70s. His family had settled in Greenville, New York. There, he'd married and fathered a son, Horst Jr., born in 1987, and a daughter, born in October 1988. Horst and Horst Jr. were particularly close. In fact, it would be more accurate to say, inseparable. The little boy went everywhere with his dad. He could often be seen buckled into the passenger seat of his father's pickup as they drove around town together. It was a standing joke in the family that where you saw Big Horst, you saw Little Horst.

January 23, 1989, was the eve of Little Horst's second birthday. It was also the day that Horst Sr. received a frantic early morning call from a friend. The man was out of town on business and was concerned about his wife. Her office had just called to let him know that she hadn't shown up for work that day. Would Horst do a driveby to check on her? Horst, of course, said yes. Little Horst wanted to go with his father but since he was still in his pajamas and hadn't had his breakfast yet, he was told that he'd have to stay behind. The little boy was teary-eyed as his dad drove away from the house without him. Later, everyone in the Eppenbach family would be thankful for that small mercy.

The woman who Horst had agreed to check on, lived just two miles along Route 6 in Deerpark, New York. Horst was at the house in minutes, noticing as he pulled up that the woman's car was still in the drive. That was a good thing. Most likely she was just feeling a bit under the weather and had decided to stay in bed. Horst parked his truck and crossed the lawn. He knocked at the front door and waited. Nothing. Then he knocked again and now he heard footsteps approaching. In the next moment, the door swung open and Horst found himself facing a masked man. The man was holding a shotgun. Without uttering a word, he pulled the trigger, firing off three rapid shots that took Horst in the chest. At that close range, he never stood a chance. Little Horst would never see his beloved dad again.

The perpetrator of this vicious crime wasn't exactly new to this. He knew about trace evidence and how to avoid leaving any behind. Before leaving the house, he wiped the place down, picked up the shotgun wadding, and collected all of his cigarette butts. Then he drove away in Horst's red pickup, later abandoning the vehicle behind the old Middletown drive-in on Route 17. The murder would be uncovered when a police officer arrived at the house, sent there by the concerned husband after he did not hear back from Horst. The woman would be found tied to her bed, alive but extremely traumatized, having been subjected to a brutal rape. She could tell the police nothing about her attacker. He'd worn a mask throughout, she said. His only distinguishing feature was his voice, which was exceptionally deep.

That was hardly enough to build a murder inquiry on. The Greenville police worked the case hard, but they were swimming upstream from the start. There was no physical evidence, no one who had seen or heard anything. There was, of course, a semen sample, retrieved while performing the rape kit on the victim, but that was of limited use. DNA profiling was only just coming to the fore as a forensic tool. Although a profile was extracted, there was nothing to compare it to. CODIS was still several years away. It was hardly a surprise when the investigation ran into trouble. At this stage, there appeared little chance of resolution, little chance of justice for Horst Eppenbach's grieving family.

Ten years on and half a country away in the small town of Calhan, Colorado, there was another vicious crime, one that bore startling similarities to the Deerpark rape. A woman was attacked in her home, tied up, and repeatedly violated. She was unable to describe her assailant since he'd worn a mask. All she would say was that he spoke in a deep voice. Other clues, fingerprints, and the like, were non-existent, although semen was retrieved from the victim. There was also the means to test it now and a profile was duly extracted. Submitted to CODIS, it returned a match, not to an individual but to an unsolved homicide. The murder of Horst Eppenbach.

The investigation into Eppenbach's death had now lain dormant for over a decade. But the link to an active investigation rejuvenated it. Meanwhile, in Colorado, investigators had identified a rape suspect, a seldom-employed laborer named Peter McGrath. Greenville detectives were interested to note that McGrath was a New York native and that he'd been living in a labor hostel in Deerpark at the time of the Eppenbach slaying. This was just a short walk from the crime scene. During the intervening years, McGrath had lived in Matamoros and Port Jervis, New York, in New Jersey, and in Peyton, Colorado. And everywhere he landed, mayhem followed.

Peter McGrath had begun his criminal career early, racking up his first arrest at the age of just 13. He would grow into a mean-spirited drunk, 6'2" of bottled-up anger, ready to unleash his fury on anyone who annoyed him. His current rap sheet listed sixteen arrests, most for crimes of violence, and most leading to convictions. There was a fight in a Port Jervis bar where he beat a man within an inch of his life in a dispute over what to play on a jukebox. There was an altercation with his former girlfriend when he'd threatened to murder her and their 11-month-old daughter. There was the 1987 rape of a Greenville woman, and now this latest sexual assault in Colorado.

And, of course, there was the rape in Deerpark, and the murder of Horst Eppenbach. McGrath hadn't been charged with those crimes yet, but the investigators knew instinctively that they had their man. McGrath was placed under surveillance. Before long, detectives had collected several cigarette butts that their suspect had discarded. These were brought to New York, where a profile was extracted and compared to the semen from the Deerpark crime scene. No one was really surprised when there was a match. The odds of anyone other than Peter McGrath having committed the crimes were calculated at 280 billion to one.

But McGrath was not about to submit meekly to justice. Arrested and confined to the El Paso County Jail, he put up a legal battle against extradition to New York. Such motions seldom succeed though, and McGrath was eventually shipped back east to answer for his crimes. He appeared for trial at the Orange County Court in May 2001, charged with second-degree murder. McGrath entered a not guilty plea, but the evidence was against him. It took the jury just 90 minutes to convict. He was sentenced to 25 years to life. Several detectives who'd worked the case over its 12-year span, stated afterward that they wished it could have been the death penalty.

But that was not an option in the state of New York and so Horst Eppenbach's family will have to be satisfied with the fact that his killer will be viewing the world from behind prison bars for the foreseeable future. There is no closure in a murder case, not for the family of the victim.

Several of Horst Eppenbach's kin were in the courtroom to see his killer sent to prison but Horst Jr., Little Horst, was not among them. He couldn't bear to be in the same room with the man who'd taken his beloved father away from him. As a two-year-old, Horst Jr. had been fond of following his dad around the house, totting his toy toolbox, insistent on helping his dad with his maintenance chores. Where you saw Big Horst, you saw Little Horst, the family used to say. Never again.

Repertoire of Lies

Up until the age of 55, Jane Alexander had lived a life of domestic quietude. Born in San Francisco in 1922, Jane had attended Notre Dame High School and Lone Mountain College, before joining the intelligence branch of the Navy during World War II. It was while in the service that she met her husband Albert, a banker. The couple married in 1945 and would enjoy 32 happy years together, during which they raised six children. In 1968, the family set up home in a comfortable residence in San Anselmo. But just nine years later, this golden age came to an abrupt end. Albert collapsed and died of a heart attack, leaving Jane a widow in her mid-50s.

Albert had been Jane's soulmate. She took his death hard, descending into a deep depression that would hover over her like a dark cloud for the next three years. Then, in 1980, an old family friend showed up on the scene. Tom O'Donnell was handsome and charismatic and well-traveled. He had a large circle of friends and he was an excellent raconteur, entertaining everyone he met with tales of his exploits as an international mover and shaker.

Tom's travels had frequently taken him off the beaten track. His favorite after-dinner stories had to do with his many close calls in politically unstable third-world countries. The way Tom told it, made him sound like a latter-day James Bond. Jane found herself falling for him and in just a few months they'd started dating. Soon he'd moved into her San Anselmo home. Jane had never imagined that she could be happy again after Albert's death. The next three years would prove her wrong.

Then, in October 1983, another tragedy. Jane's beloved aunt,
Gertrude McCabe, was murdered in her home in San Jose. Not just
murdered, savaged. The frail 88-year-old had been bludgeoned
with a blunt instrument, stabbed 27 times, throttled, suffocated
with a pillow. Finally, the killer had twisted a bicycle lock chain
around her slim throat and choked her to death. This was an
incredibly callous murder, perpetrated against a tiny, defenseless,
woman who barely topped 5-foot and weighed just 97 pounds.

Who would commit such a terrible crime? And why? Initially, the
police believed that this was a robbery gone wrong. The McCabe
residence had been ransacked, with drawers pulled out and
clothes strewn about the place. But as detectives dug a little
deeper, they quickly realized that this was no burglary. There
were valuable items in the house, jewelry left on a countertop,
cash in the dead woman's purse. None of it had been taken. The
only thing missing was the registry for Gertrude's checkbook,
which she usually kept in a bedside drawer.

So this wasn't a burglary after all, but a poorly executed attempt to
emulate one. That pointed to a killer who was known to the victim
and gave the police another question to ponder. Who benefitted
from Gertrude McCabe's death? The answer to that question was
easy. The main benefactor of Gertrude's estate was her niece, Jane
Alexander.

Was it possible that Jane Alexander might be behind the killing of
her beloved Aunt Gert? Jane who'd appeared so distraught and

who'd wept so bitterly on receiving the news? Unlikely as that seemed, a look into Jane Alexander's finances suggested a powerful motive. Jane was broke, having blown through a small fortune over the prior three years. Recently, she'd taken out a $200,000 second mortgage on her house and it was unclear how she was going to service that debt. Her checking account was all but empty.

All of this made Jane Alexander a strong suspect. Still, investigators were all but certain that it wasn't she who'd wielded the blade, or the bludgeon, or the bicycle chain. Women seldom kill in such a brutal fashion. The signs pointed to a male perpetrator. If Jane Alexander was indeed involved, then she'd recruited someone else to do the killing for her. That someone was likely to be Tom O'Donnell.

Over the year that followed, investigators continued to monitor their prime suspects. They believed they'd cracked their case and were just waiting for Alexander and O'Donnell to slip up and give them the evidence they needed for an arrest. Before that moment arrived, however, Tom O'Donnell was gone. He slipped away on the night of June 7, 1984, leaving Jane a 12-page letter. In it, he explained that some old business partners had tracked him down and were seeking revenge for a shady diamond deal gone wrong. His life was in danger, he said, and hers might be too if he stayed around her. He'd therefore decided to go into hiding.

Tom O'Donnell had always been a gifted liar. During the three years that he and Jane had been together, he'd spun such an intricate web of lies that Jane was totally and utterly in the dark as to his true intentions. Now, with Tom out of the picture and unable to maintain the charade, it all came crashing in on her. He'd been playing her, leeching away her cash and assets, putting the money into dodgy business deals and 'surefire' stock trades that inevitably tanked. She was broke, her nest egg gone, her house heavily mortgaged. Tom O'Donnell had played her right until the end. On the day he disappeared, he'd convinced her to hand over her last $10,000 to him.

It would be fair to ask how an adult woman, especially one of Jane Alexander's years, could have been so utterly duped. But you should remember that Jane had been married to a banker for over three decades. Albert had taken care of the finances and Jane had been happy to leave such matters to him. When it came to money, she was a babe in the woods. Aside from that, she was in love with Tom O'Donnell and believed he loved her too. It had never crossed her mind that he might cheat her.

But now Jane was riled, determined to track O'Donnell down and haul him before the courts to answer for his misdeeds. That determination only increased when she received a second letter from him, five months after he went missing. O'Donnell was spinning his lies again, telling her that he'd made peace with his former business partners and was now working for them. Jane didn't believe a word of it. She started calling around to her former lover's friends. They were less than forthcoming but Jane could read between the lines and eventually determined that Tom was in San Jose. She passed on what she knew to the police, and they did the rest. O'Donnell was arrested at the home of his latest victim, a wealthy widow who he'd drawn in with his usual repertoire of lies.

Tom O'Donnell was eventually convicted on four counts of fraud and sentenced to four years in prison. It was justice, of a kind, but it did nothing to alleviate his former girlfriend's financial plight. Jane was bankrupt, forced to sell her house and to find a job for the first time in her life. She ended up living in an unheated apartment and working as a receptionist in a retirement home. She also wasn't done yet with Tom O'Donnell. She was convinced now, as was the San Anselmo Police Department, that O'Donnell was responsible for the murder of Gertrude McCabe. Now, she was determined to prove it.

And so, Jane Alexander took on a new persona, that of amateur sleuth. She began gathering up every piece of evidence she could, spending months digging through police reports and financial records. Finally, two important clues jumped out at her. The first had to do with a call that O'Donnell made to relatives in Montana on the day that Gertrude McCabe died. He'd told them he would soon be able to repay the $10,000 he owed them. Jane's aunt had just died, he said, and she was about to receive a substantial inheritance. The problem was in the timing of this call. At the time it was made, Gertrude's body had not yet been discovered.

The second clue came from a conversation O'Donnell had with Jane's daughter-in-law, Rocky, soon after the murder. He'd told her that Gertrude had been garroted. This was true, of course, but the information had never been made public. There was only one way that O'Donnell could have known.

While Jane Alexander was unearthing these anomalies in the case, San Anselmo detectives made a breakthrough of their own. This one had to do with Gertrude's checkbook register, the only item missing from the crime scene. The police had believed at the time that the killer had taken it to determine how much Gertrude was worth. But the register would turn up a few weeks after the murder. Jane and Tom were going through the house, finalizing Gertrude's affairs, when Tom "found" the missing register. He said that it had been in the bedside drawer where it was usually kept. Unfortunately for Tom, this did not tie in with the crime scene photographs. These showed the drawer in question pulled out, with no sign of the missing register. The only way it could have ended up in the drawer was if Tom had placed it there.

This was powerful circumstantial evidence. Yet there was still one major obstacle for investigators to overcome. Tom O'Donnell had a seemingly unbreakable alibi. On the day that Gertrude McCabe was killed, he'd been out of town, staying with a friend in Burbank. He'd only returned to San Anselmo the following morning. That meant that he could not have committed the murder.

Or did it? Checking the mileage O'Donnell had covered in his rental car, detectives discovered that he'd done 669 miles that day, almost the exact distance of a roundtrip between Burbank and Gertrude McCabe's home in San Jose. The alibi was blown. It was time for Tom O'Donnell to pay the piper.

It had taken nine years for the San Anselmo police, with the considerable help of Jane Alexander, to build its case against Tom O'Donnell. O'Donnell was taken into custody in Los Angeles on

March 17, 1992, and charged with first-degree murder. Convicted on that charge, he was sentenced to 25 years to life in prison. O'Donnell was eligible for parole in 2007 but was denied at that time. He would not have another hearing. He died behind bars in 2010.

For Jane Alexander, the arrest and conviction of her former boyfriend was the start of a whole new chapter of her life. After the trial, Jane co-founded Citizens Against Homicide, with her friend Jan Miller. The group's goal is to provide support to the families of murder victims, to help them keep up the pressure on the authorities in cold and unsolved cases, and to keep killers behind bars once they are caught. In 2006, Jane Alexander received the Minerva Award, honoring women who have achieved extraordinary things. She would continue her work until her death in December 2008, at the age of 86. At that time, the organization she had founded was looking into nearly 500 unsolved homicides.

Goodbye, Krystal Jean

Kevin Smith

In the Gulf Coast town of Texas City, Texas, 13-year-old Krystal Jean Baker had a unique claim to fame. She was the great-niece of Norma Jean Baker, better known to the world as Marilyn Monroe. Krystal's connection to the Hollywood icon came via her paternal bloodline. And she had other things in common with her famous aunt. She was pretty and blonde and talented. Her teenage ambition was to join the cheerleading squad once she started high school.

But Krystal Jean would never get the opportunity to cheer the Stingarees onto the playing fields at Texas City High School, or to achieve any of the things she hoped for in life. That is because, on Tuesday, March 2, 1996, Krystal Jean Baker would be dead, her body discarded under a bridge on the banks of the Trinity River.

That Tuesday should have been a normal day for Krystal. But she woke complaining of an earache and so her mom, Jeannie, agreed that she could take the day off school. Jeannie didn't want her youngest home alone, though, and so she sent her to her grandmother's house, just down the street.

Krystal would spend the morning dozing on the couch. By early afternoon, all symptoms of the earache were gone. In fact, she felt so much better that when a friend called and asked if she wanted to hang out, she said yes without even asking her grandma. That would spark an argument between the two of them during which Krystal stormed off. Her friend's house was just a short walk away. Krystal never arrived.

Jeannie was furious when she got home from work and heard of her daughter's insolence and disobedience. She was ready to have it out with Krystal, the minute that she walked through the door. But as the hours ticked by with no sign of the teenager, Jeannie's anger began to morph into concern. At 7 p.m., she called the friend who'd phoned Krystal that afternoon, only to learn that Krystal had never shown up. None of Krystal's other friends had heard from her either. Panicking now, Jeannie and her family hit the streets and began a search, a search that became more frantic with each passing minute. Finding no trace of Krystal in any of the places she might have been, Jeannie eventually went to the police and reported her daughter missing.

What the distraught mother did not know at that time was that Krystal had already been found. A call had come into the police station at around 5 p.m. that afternoon, reporting the discovery of a body under the Trinity River Bridge. The officer who responded to the scene found a middle-aged couple sitting in their pickup, clearly in shock. The man identified himself as Gerald Barnes and said that it was he who had made the 911 call. He and his wife, Joyce, had spent the day fishing, he told the officer, and had found the body when they returned to their truck. They'd covered it with a blanket, "out of respect." The officer then went to inspect the corpse and found that it was a young girl. Ligature marks around her throat suggested that she'd been strangled; blood on her panties pointed to a sexual assault. By the time that backup arrived at the scene, the police already knew who they'd found. Krystal Baker's act of disobedience had cost her life.

Right from the start, it was clear that this was going to be a difficult crime to solve. Krystal had not been killed where she was found and there were scant clues at the scene. Despite the recovery of biological material, the technology of the day was not advanced enough to extract a DNA profile. There was also a decided lack of suspects although the police did focus for a brief time on the couple who had made the gruesome discovery. After they were cleared, investigators zeroed in on Krystal's boyfriend, Brandon Lowe, a recent arrival from Dallas. That scrutiny only increased when they learned that the baby-faced Lowe had lied to Krystal about his age. He was actually a 21-year-old man.

But Lowe insisted that he and Krystal had been friends, nothing more. He also had an alibi and he agreed to take a polygraph, which he passed. That didn't strike him from the suspect list, but he was looking less likely. The police had little else to go on. After a local trucker was assessed and eventually cleared as a person of interest, the case went cold.

A year passed. Then, in March 1997, another young girl was dead. Laura Smithers was the same age as Krystal and the circumstances of her death were strikingly similar. She had disappeared from a suburban street in broad daylight and her body was found in a rural location, next to water, just 30 minutes from where Krystal had been dumped. She had also been raped and strangled. Those commonalities led investigators to consider a frightening possibility. Was it possible that they had a serial killer in the area, a killer whose preferred prey was young girls?

This is by no means an outlandish idea. Just across the bay from Texas City lies Galveston. It forms the southernmost point of a corridor that has become known as the 'Texas Killing Fields.' Spanning I-45 along a 50-mile stretch from Houston to the Gulf, this is an area with a macabre reputation. Since the 1970s, it has been a repository for the bodies of homicide victims, as many as 40 of them, with many of the cases still unsolved. Were Krystal Baker and Laura Smithers the latest names to be added to that deadly roll? The police couldn't say for certain, but it was a possibility. And if it was the case, then the murders of the two teenagers had just gotten exponentially more difficult to solve. In fact, they would remain unresolved for the next decade-and-a-half.

In 2010, almost 14 years after Krystal Baker's murder, the Chambers County Sherriff's Office decided to take a fresh look at the case. The obvious place to begin their new investigation was with the DNA evidence. Technology had moved on over the intervening years. The cops were hoping that the crime lab could extract a DNA profile from the clothes Krystal had been wearing at the time of her death. The items were therefore sent to the lab for analysis. The news that came back was good. The lab had detected a semen stain on Krystal's panties and had extracted a profile from it.

Brandon Lowe, by now a man in his mid-thirties, must have been surprised when the police knocked on his door and asked him to submit to a DNA swab. After all these years, and in spite of his passed polygraph, Brandon remained the preferred suspect of the investigative team. But DNA would clear him. Whoever had killed Krystal, it wasn't Brandon.

Next, the profile was submitted to CODIS, the national database containing the profiles of millions of convicted felons. Within just a couple of days, it returned a match. The man whose profile they'd lifted was 45-year-old Kevin Edison Smith, an individual whose rap sheet looked like a checklist for every transgression in the Texas Penal Code. Up until that point, the investigative team had never heard of him, nor connected him to the Krystal Baker homicide.

Galveston native Kevin Smith wasn't difficult to locate. He was currently on parole from his latest period of incarceration, working as a welder at a Port Arthur oil refinery. Chambers County detectives immediately set off on the two-hour drive and arrested Smith at his place of work. Confronted with allegations of murder, he was vehement in his denials, claiming that he had never even heard of Krystal Jean Baker. The DNA evidence said different.

But is DNA really infallible? Just as investigators were congratulating themselves on finally cracking the cold case, they got word of another potential suspect. Lorenzo Sanchez was an even more despicable character than Kevin Smith. He was currently serving a life term in Minnesota, for knifing to death a ten-year-old girl. The tip-off came from a retired FBI agent, who'd heard from an informant that Sanchez had been boasting to his fellow inmates that he was the one who'd killed Krystal Jean Baker.

Criminals, of course, do this kind of thing all the time, bigging themselves up by claiming responsibility for high-profile crimes. Was that the case here? Was the DNA evidence wrong? Was Kevin Smith innocent? Or had he and Sanchez worked together to snuff out Krystal's young life?

The answer to all of these questions was no. Sanchez was lying about his involvement in the murder. He hadn't even been in Texas at the time it was committed. As investigators had expected, he was trying to gain a degree of infamy by attaching himself to a famous case.

The focus was now firmly back on Kevin Smith and things did not look good for him. Prosecutors had stated their intention of seeking the death penalty. It was to avoid that sanction that Smith eventually cracked and decided to come clean. His confession was delivered in a self-pitying tone, almost as though he were the real victim.

According to Smith, he was driving in Texas City when he spotted Krystal walking. He pulled up beside her, rolled down his window, and offered her a ride. Krystal, however, turned him down. Smith then cast his gaze up and down the street and realized that the two of them were the only people around. He decided on the spur of the moment to abduct her. Jumping from the vehicle he grabbed Krystal and started dragging her toward the passenger door.

Krystal did not go easy. She put up a fight. But Smith was a big and powerful man, more than a match for a petite 13-year-old. Krystal was pulled into the car, throttled and beaten into submission, violently raped. Smith could have stopped there, thrown the teenager out of the vehicle, and raced away from the scene. Instead, he picked up a welding strap, wrapped it around Krystal's neck and pulled it tight, cutting off her breath. He was probably looking directly into the child's eyes when the light faded from them.

And yet, Smith bizarrely claimed at his 2012 trial that he hadn't meant to kill Krystal. He offered his sniveling account with tears in his eyes, pleading for his own life when he placed so little value on the lives of others. In the end, he succeeded, avoiding the needle, and receiving life without parole instead. That was a bittersweet victory for Krystal's family. Jeannie Escamilla had declared herself ready and willing to witness the execution of the man who'd stolen her daughter's life. At least, Kevin Smith will never have the chance to inflict that agony on anyone else's family. He will die behind bars.

FOOTNOTE:

Kevin Smith was cleared of the murder of Laura Smithers, which remains unsolved. So too, most of the dozens of homicides related to the Texas Killing Fields.

Traces of Death

On the night before she died, Kay Sybers went to dinner with her husband at the Sealander Restaurant in Panama City, Florida. The 52-year-old was in jovial mood that night, and with good reason. She and her husband, William, lived a gilded life. He was the chief medical examiner of Florida's 14th Judicial District and a founding partner in Bay Pathology, a renowned medical lab in the area. Home was a large, upscale mansion on Gulf Drive, overlooking the Gulf of Mexico. Kay had raised the couple's three children there and had made a fine job of it. All three were now pursuing graduate and post-grad educations. The younger two, Timothy and Jennifer, were currently home from college, adding to Kay's good mood. On the night of May 29, 1991, everything seemed right in the Sybers universe.

William and Kay arrived home from their dinner date at around 11:30 p.m. Timothy was still up, and he and his mom talked for a while, reminiscing about old times. William went straight to bed and was already asleep when Kay joined him in the bedroom. She swallowed a single Doral sleeping pill and then slipped under the covers. She was soon asleep.

It was around 4:30 a.m. when Dr. William Sybers was shaken awake by his wife. Kay was complaining of chest pains and an ache in her left arm. Since these are potential indicators of a cardiac problem, William suggested that they drive to the local hospital. However, Kay refused, and William didn't push her on the issue. He knew that she was an intensely private person. She'd told him frequently in the past that she refused to be examined by a doctor in Panama City since most of them were in the Sybers' social circle. And so, William made his wife comfortable and then attempted to draw some blood from her arm, so that he could test it when he got to the lab later that day. However, he inexplicably botched the blood draw, something he'd done thousands of times during his storied medical career. He ended up applying a band-aid to the puncture wound and throwing the used syringe into the trash.

Kay Sybers was still resting when her husband left for his office at 6:30 that morning. On the way in, he tried contacting his partner, Dr. Stephen McClellan but was unable to reach him. Over the next three hours, Dr. Sybers made several calls to his residence, all of which went unanswered. Eventually, just before nine, there was a call from his daughter, Jennifer, saying that she had tried waking her mother and was unable to do so. Dr. Sybers told her to put her brother, Timothy, on the phone. He instructed Timothy, a medical student, to check on his mother and report back. The feedback wasn't promising. Timothy said simply that his mom "didn't look good." He was told to sit tight, that help was on the way.

The next call that Dr. Sybers made that day was to Dan Harris, one of his assistants at the medical examiner's office. He wanted Harris to go to his house and check on his wife. Harris departed immediately, taking another assistant, Bill Johnson, with him. They arrived at 10:54 and were let in by a frantic Jennifer. Kay Sybers was lying in her bed, unconscious and with no discernible pulse. Harris and Johnson immediately started cardiopulmonary resuscitation, but it was already too late. Johnson would later say that Mrs. Sybers had probably been dead for two to three hours by the time they got there.

Now followed a frenetic few minutes, during which an ambulance and a Bay County Sheriff's Deputy arrived at the house. Johnson sent the officer on his way, saying that they had the situation under control. There was no need for the ambulance either, Kay Sybers was beyond help. Instead, after a consultation with his boss, Johnson placed a call to the Southerland Funeral Home. Dr. Sybers was explicit in his instructions. He did not want his wife to be autopsied. He wanted her embalmed immediately, in accordance with her wishes. Undertaker John Williams wasn't about to argue with the Chief Medical Examiner of the 14th Judicial District. He got to work immediately, completing the process by 2:30 a.m.

Within just a few hours of her death, Kay Sybers had been removed to the funeral home; her body had been drained of bodily fluids; the embalming process had been completed; preparations were underway to ship her remains back to her hometown of Fort Dodge, Iowa, for burial. To some, that might have seemed disrespectfully hasty.

But then came the phone call, placed by Dr. Terrence Steiner to the Florida Department of Law Enforcement (FDLE) in Panama City. Steiner was a former colleague of Dr. Sybers and had some dirt on him. He reported that Sybers was a serial philanderer and that he was currently involved in a long-term extramarital affair with one of his co-workers, a lab technician named Judy Ray. Taken with his wife's unexpected death, the refusal of an autopsy, and the inordinately hasty embalming of the corpse, that was enough to raise suspicion.

The following morning, Dr. William Sybers answered a knock at his front door and found FDLE agents Scott Sanderson and Mike Klages standing on the step. Sybers welcomed them inside and spent the next 40 minutes answering questions. He said that his wife had been complaining of chest pains for the last 18 months and that he suspected she might have been borderline diabetic. He'd begged her to see a doctor, but she'd consistently refused. He also told the investigators that Kay did not have life insurance and that he would not benefit financially from her death. As for extramarital affairs, he insisted that such stories were just vicious rumors. Sybers was then asked if he'd consent to an independent autopsy on his wife's remains. He agreed.

William Sybers had remained calm and cooperative throughout that initial interview. He'd also been somewhat economical with the truth. As investigators started to delve into his background, they began to unearth some deep, dark secrets about the good doctor.

The first of those was that Sybers was lying about his relationship with Judy Ray. Phone records showed that the two of them were in constant communication, exchanging hundreds of calls in the three months prior to Kay Sybers' death. In fact, Dr. Sybers had called Ray at 6:36 a.m. on the day his wife died. He'd called her again, just minutes after his initial interview with Agents Sanderson and Klages. Judy Ray would later admit to a sexual relationship, although she insisted that it only started after Kay's death. The phone records suggest otherwise.

But sexual indiscretions were not the only misdeeds that the FDLE investigators would dredge up. Dr. Sybers was also guilty of misusing his prescription pad, writing as many as 130 suspicious prescriptions over a four-year period. These were for a variety of drugs, including Valium, amphetamine-type diet pills, and powerful painkillers. Some he prescribed for his wife, others for employees at his lab. These same employees were used to collect the drugs from several pharmacies in the Panama City area. What is clear, however, is that these drugs seldom, if ever, reached the named patient. Most were handed over directly to Dr. Sybers. One former colleague told investigators that Sybers showed clear indications of someone who was abusing amphetamines. The allegation was never proven.

What was proven, however, was that Dr. Sybers had abused his position of responsibility. That brought a sanction from the Florida Department of Professional Regulation. The punishment was little more than a slap on the wrist, a $3,000 fine, plus 20 hours of mandatory training in medical record keeping and risk management.

So, Dr. Sybers was guilty of medical misconduct and had been sanctioned accordingly. But what of the more serious allegations against him? What of the suggestion that he'd caused his wife's death? That was far more difficult to prove, due to the condition of the body when received for autopsy. All the blood and urine had been flushed and replaced by embalming fluid. With it had gone any trace of toxins or drugs that might have been present. The pathologists did determine, however, that Kay Sybers did not have a heart condition. She'd been in generally good health. Her cause of death was a mystery.

And this was a mystery that would defy resolution. After a 15-month investigation, the Florida Department of Law Enforcement was forced to concede defeat. There was no evidence to support the notion that William Sybers had killed his wife. Panama City State Attorney James Appleman confirmed this, stating on record that there appeared to be no case to pursue. The matter would be revisited in January 1993, when Florida Governor Lawton Chiles appointed a special prosecutor to reexamine the evidence. But Dr. Sybers refused permission for the exhumation of his wife's remains and was supported in that refusal by Kay's family. The investigation floundered.

William Sybers was free to continue his life. However, the shadow of death would continue to stalk him. In February 1993, his son Timothy committed suicide by shooting himself in the head at the family's vacation home in Wisconsin. Timothy had been deeply affected by his mother's death and had told a friend that he could not live with the knowledge that his father had murdered his mother.

Putting this latest tragedy behind him, William Sybers married his former mistress, Judy Ray, in 1994. That same year, he retired from medical practice. He and the new Mrs. Syders would spend the next 24 months living aboard their yacht, cruising the Florida coastline and the Caribbean Islands. Thereafter, they settled in Victoria, in British Colombia, Canada. At this time, there was no inkling that the death of his first wife would ever come back to haunt him.

But then there was Dr. Michael Swango. Swango was a serial killer, responsible for at least four murders, and possibly as many as 60. His favored method was to inject his victims with succinylcholine, a paralyzing drug usually given to patients before surgery. Death by an overdose of this drug is painful and protracted. The lungs are impaired, the victim struggles to breathe, and slowly suffocates. Thereafter, the drug breaks down rapidly in the body, leaving no trace.

It was partially in response to the Swango case that National Medical Services, a lab based in Willow Grove, Pennsylvania, developed a groundbreaking new technique to find traces of succinylcholine. The drug itself may dissipate but it leaves behind a chemical signature that can be detected long after the fact. Now, Florida investigators wondered if the same test could be applied to the organs they had harvested from Kay Sybers. The answer to that question was yes. There were clear indicators of the presence of succinylcholine. There was only one way that the drug could have entered Kay Sybers' system.

Arrested and charged, Dr. William Sybers went on trial in March 2001, with the prosecution arguing that he'd murdered his wife so that he'd be free to marry his mistress without giving up half of his $6 million fortune. Sybers' expensively assembled defense team countered by challenging the results of the lab tests, leaning heavily on reasonable doubt. The jury rejected that argument, taking less than six hours to find Williams Sybers guilty of murder. He was sentenced to 15 years to life, but the conviction was overturned two years later in 2003. At that time, the doctor was offered a deal. He could plead to manslaughter and walk free with time served, or he could put himself through another murder trial. Perhaps understandably, he took the deal.

But William Sybers would go through the rest of his life insisting that he took the deal only because it was the most convenient thing to do. He was not responsible for his wife's death, he claimed. Does he have a case? Perhaps, but one would have to stretch credulity to accept it. Too many questions remained unanswered.

How is it possible that he, a trained and highly experienced doctor, could have 'botched' the drawing of blood from his wife? Was that story not just invented to explain the presence of puncture wounds on Kay's arms? Given his background in pathology, why would he have so carelessly disposed of a used syringe? Was it so that the syringe could not be tested? Why did he, the Chief Medical Examiner of the district, go against protocol and refuse an autopsy? Why was he in such a hurry to have his wife's body embalmed? Most importantly, why was the chemical signature of succinylcholine detected in her organs? These are questions that neither Dr. William Sybers nor his supporters can answer.

William Sybers died of lung cancer at his home in Clearwater Beach, Florida on April 19, 2014. He was 81 years old.

Hide in Plain Sight

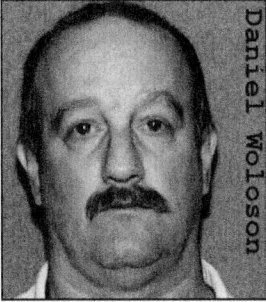

Carbondale, Illinois is unique among its rural neighbors. The small, Midwestern town is home to Southern Illinois University and its 20,000 students make up the bulk of its population. The SIU campus is a sprawling property, with various buildings connected by pathways, some of which pass through dense woodland. There is even a railroad track and several streams that cut through.

In the summer of 1981, media studies major Susan Schumake was in her senior year at SIU. The 21-year-old lived off campus, in a house she shared with three roommates. Susan also worked at WIDB, the campus radio station. On the afternoon of August 17, she had a meeting scheduled with colleagues from the station. That meeting was arranged for 3:00 p.m. at the Student Center. Thereafter, Susan was going to meet one of her roommates for dinner.

At around 3:00 a.m. on the morning of Tuesday, August 18, the SIU campus police received a frantic phone call. On the line was Susan

Schumake's roommate, the same roommate with whom Susan had the dinner date. Except, Susan hadn't shown, and her friend had been unable to contact her since. This was highly unusual since Susan was an ultra-dependable person, a stickler for punctuality. Her friend was concerned that something might have happened to her.

Campus police forces deal with this type of call all the time. Almost always, the missing student shows up of his or her own accord, usually within a couple of hours. This, however, was not one of those cases. When Susan had still not returned to her digs by breakfast, officers were dispatched to search for her. They soon learned that her meeting had been moved from the Student Center to another building, Wright Hall. That meant that Susan would have had to walk back to the Student Center to meet her friend for dinner. The path she'd have taken was particularly overgrown and was jokingly called the Ho Chi Minh Trail by students. This was where the officers now focused their search.

And it wasn't long before they noticed something untoward. Along a section of the route, the undergrowth had been flattened, as though someone had blundered through. A campus officer followed the path into the bushes. About 40 feet in, he came across the body of a young woman, her jeans and panties pulled down around her ankles, her eyes staring blankly at the sky. Susan Schumake had been found. This was now a matter for the Carbondale Police Department.

Reconstructing the crime wasn't difficult. Susan had obviously been ambushed along the path, dragged into the bushes, subdued by strangulation, raped. What was unclear was whether she was unconscious or already dead when the sexual assault took place. Either way, this was a terrible, brutal murder, one that caused considerable alarm in the college town. On a campus where there were thousands of young women, might the killer strike again?

Under immense pressure to solve the crime, the Carbondale police started with the victim. Was there anyone in Susan's life who might have meant her harm? Her roommates said no. Susan was outgoing, friendly, considerate. She did not have an enemy in the world. Had anyone been bothering her? Again, the answer was no. The petite, pretty student did have an ex-boyfriend, but their parting had been amicable. The ex was not a suspect in any case since he'd been out of state when the murder happened. The police then expanded the scope of their investigation to look at known sex offenders living in the area. That was when the name of John Paul Phillips first came up.

Phillips was a lowlife, a habitual criminal with a long history of violent offenses against women. He'd recently been released from a prison term for a 1976 attack on a young woman and her boyfriend. The couple had survived but Phillips was also a suspect in the rapes and murders of 22-year-old Theresa Clark and 24-year-old Kathleen McSharry, both SIU students. These unfortunate women had been knifed to death in the year before Phillips was sent to prison. At the time, the police still lacked the forensic evidence to link Phillips to the murders. Might he be up to his old tricks again? Might he have killed Susan Schumake?

Questioned at his father's construction business, Phillips denied involvement in Susan Schumake's death. There was good reason for the police to disbelieve him. For starters, Phillips had fresh scratches on his face. In addition, he admitted that he had been on the SIU campus on the day that Susan was killed. However, he had ready explanations for both the scratches and for his presence on campus. The scratches had been sustained while playing with a friend's dog and he'd been at SIU working on one of his father's construction projects. Phillips was then asked to provide hair samples for comparison with two hairs that had been lifted from Susan Schumake's body. He complied willingly.

With the hairs sent to the lab for comparison, detectives called on Phillips's friend, to verify his explanation for the scratches. The friend said that he was lying. The dog had not scratched him. This was hardly a surprise to investigators. They were sure that they had their man, convinced that the hairs would prove it.

Unfortunately, it would not be that simple. The hairs did not match. John Paul Phillips was off the hook even if many at the Carbondale Police Department still believed that he was the man who'd done it. Then, just as investigators were fretting over their case slipping away from them, there was a new development. Maintenance staff had found a red tote bag, hidden in the weeds on the SIU campus, about 400 yards from where Susan Schumake had been found. Inside was a vial of prescription medication, made out to a man named Daniel Woloson.

Like John Paul Phillips, Daniel Woloson had a long rap sheet. Unlike Phillips, he was not a violent criminal. Woloson was mainly a burglar and an inept one at that. He'd been in and out of prison and had only recently been released from his latest stint in the pen.

Woloson wasn't difficult to find. He was living in a low-rent motel in town. Questioned by police, he admitted that the bag was his. He said that he'd hidden it where it was found. According to Woloson, he'd been down on his luck after his release from prison and had been sleeping out in the open, under a bridge on the SIU campus. This, of course, put him close to the crime scene although Woloson swore that he'd had nothing to do with Susan Schumake's death. He, too, provided hairs for comparison. No one was really surprised when the results came back negative. Woloson did not seem the type. John Paul Phillips remained a far more likely suspect.

Three months passed, three fear-filled months for the SIU corpus, three frustrating months for the Carbondale police. Then, in November 1981, another woman was dead. The body of Joan Wetherall was found in a stream just north of town. The 30-year-old waitress had been beaten and strangled. She had also been raped. It did not take a genius to figure out that the M.O. was near identical to that in the Schumake murder. That raised a terrifying possibility. Was there a serial killer on the streets of Carbondale?

Just one month after the murder of Joan Wetherall, a Brazilian exchange student named Esperanza Pozza was snatched from a street, dragged into a car, and driven to an isolated spot outside of town. Keeping her cool, the brave woman did not resist. Instead, she went along with the rape, even pretending that she was enjoying it. That tactic probably saved her life. After the assault, the rapist drove her back to the spot where he'd abducted her and set her free. Esperanza immediately reported the assault. Unfortunately, the severely traumatized woman could not provide a detailed description of her attacker.

And he was not done yet. One month later, in nearby Carterville, 22-year-old Florence Beattie was approached by a man asking for directions. That was just a ruse to distract her, as he got her in a chokehold and started dragging her toward his truck. But the attacker had to loosen his grip as he tried to open the passenger door. Seizing her opportunity, Florence kneed him in the groin and wriggled free of his grasp. She sprinted away, running to a nearby police station where she provided a description of the attacker and of his vehicle. An alert was issued, and the would-be abductor soon apprehended. It was someone police were well-acquainted with – serial rapist and suspected serial killer, John Paul Phillips.

Phillips was charged with attempted kidnapping and would also be linked to the rape of Esperanza Pozza. Convicted of these crimes, he was sentenced to 40 years in prison. Once inside, he followed a path quite common to those of his ilk. He started bragging about other crimes he'd committed, including the still unsolved murders of Theresa Clark, Kathleen McSharry, and Joan Wetherall. It did not take long before word of these boasts reached the ears of the authorities. Phillips was then interviewed by Carbondale detectives. He wasted little time on denials.

The confessions provided by Phillips were incredibly detailed, leaving no doubt that he was indeed the person responsible for the deaths of these three women. But the one crime that Phillips would not admit to, was the murder of Susan Schumake. Despite considerable pressure by investigators, he remained adamant that she was not one of his victims. He would eventually be tried for only one homicide, that of Joan Wetherall. Convicted on that charge, he was sentenced to death. Seven years later, on November 2, 1993, John Paul Phillips suffered a massive heart attack and died in his cell.

To Susan Schumake's family, the conviction and subsequent death of John Paul Phillips provided closure. Although he'd never been convicted of killing Susan, they remained certain that he was the man responsible. The Carbondale police, though, were not so sure. Why had Phillips been so adamant in his denials of Susan's murder? What did he have to gain by those denials? Was it possible that he was telling the truth? Might the real killer still be out there?

The answer to that question lay in an evidence folder, in the two hairs that had been retrieved during the initial investigation. Each of these had a minuscule quantity of cellular material attached, far too small and far too degraded to be processed. It would take nearly 20 years for technology to eventually catch up. In the early 2000s, a method called Mini STR sampling became available, allowing forensic labs to extract a profile from samples previously considered unusable. It was thus that the Carbondale police were eventually provided with the profile of their suspect.

The first step was to compare the profile to John Paul Phillips. This was not a simple process. Phillips's DNA was not on file. It would take an exhumation order to obtain a biological sample for testing. It did not match. Next, investigators turned to the only other suspect they'd ever vetted, Daniel Woloson.

Woloson had been considered low probability during the initial investigation, mainly because violent crime had not been part of his stock in trade. But he'd since expanded his repertoire. One of his recent convictions was for the knifepoint abduction of a woman from a shopping mall. Fortunately, the victim had been able to jump out of his car when he stopped at a traffic light. Woloson had only recently been released from the prison term that the attempted abduction had earned him. He was currently living on the outskirts of Detroit, where he was working at a scrapyard.

Approached by local law enforcement to provide a DNA sample, Woloson refused. Then followed a months-long game of cat and mouse, with officers tracking Woloson, hoping that he'd discard something containing his DNA – a cigarette butt, a soda can, anything. Only, Woloson was being excessively careful, leaving nothing behind that could be used against him.

Then the police caught a break. A vehicle came into the possession of the Washtenaw County Sherriff's Office after it was used in an attempted robbery. It turned out that the car had previously belonged to Daniel Woloson. He'd only recently sold it. Examining the vehicle, officers found that the ashtray was packed with cigarette butts. What were the chances that the chain-smoking Woloson had left them there?

One of the butts was selected at random and sent to the crime lab. A DNA profile was extracted and compared against the one from the Schumake crime scene. It was a match. After 23 years, Susan Schumake's killer had been identified at last. He had been hiding in plain sight all this time.

Daniel Woloson was taken into custody on September 23, 2004. He was brought to trial in early 2006. Convicted of first-degree murder, he was sentenced to 40 years in prison, the maximum allowable under 1981 sentencing guidelines. Still, 40 years is a long time for the 45-year-old Woloson. He is unlikely to ever taste freedom again.

And that is a good thing. Investigators who worked the case are convinced that Woloson is responsible for other, as yet unsolved, homicides. Like his fellow suspect John Paul Phillips, Daniel Woloson may well be a serial killer.

For more True Crime books by Robert Keller

please visit:

http://bit.ly/kellerbooks

Printed in Great Britain
by Amazon